New Life in Luke

Lessons from the Bible which will introduce you to Jesus
And challenge you to become one of His followers

also

The Gospel of Luke

Dick Keogh

New Life in Luke

Lessons from the Bible which will introduce you to Jesus
And challenge you to become one of His followers

Copyright © Dick Keogh 2007

Scripture References are taken from the
Authorised Version of the Bible.
Quotations from the Scriptures are numbered.
These can be checked in the Scripture References Section

Also

The Gospel of Luke
(Authorised Version)

Published by
Cherith Gospel Outreach Trust
P. O. Box 15
Thurles
County Tipperary
Republic of Ireland
Web Site: www.cherithgospel.org

ISBN No. 978-0-9554736-0-9

Other Publications by the same Author

No Longer Hoping

No Longer Searching

The Clew Bay Drowning Tragedy

Saint Deirbhile and the Woman at the Well

Easter in Ireland

Three Knocks on the Door

Questions Only You Can Answer

Knock, a Light in the West

Saint Patrick – the Shamrock, the Snakes, the Sacrifice

Saint Patrick – the Slave, the Sinner, the Saint

If you would like to receive any of these, or a Bible, Free of charge,
Please write to

Cherith Gospel Outreach Trust
P. O. Box 15
Thurles
County Tipperary
Republic of Ireland

Contents

Introduction

Dear Friend,

The material for these Bible lessons is taken mainly from Luke's Gospel. However, I have quoted from other books of the Bible, including the book of Acts which was also written by Luke. As you read through the lessons you will be introduced to various people.

People you will meet

A woman who was saved at the river side.
A child with two natures.
A virgin who gave birth in a stable.
A group of downtrodden, working-class people.
Men who followed a star.
An old man who could not die until he had seen the Saviour.
A twelve-year-old girl who was raised from the dead.
A tax collector sitting in a tree.
A man who came to his senses in a pigsty.
A man who wept when he heard a cock crow.

Two Important Questions

It is my prayer that as you read the Gospel of Luke and consider the Bible lessons you will discover the answers to two very important questions. These questions were first asked when Jesus and His disciples were in a boat, crossing a lake. The first question concerns Christ and was asked by His disciples immediately after Jesus had calmed a storm on the lake. They asked, 'What manner of man is this!'[1] We live in days in which many religions and cults present a distorted picture of who Jesus really is, so it is vitally important that we discover the truth concerning Him. He Himself said, 'Ye shall know the truth, and the truth shall make you free'.[2]

Having discovered through studying the Scriptures that Jesus is the Saviour, we can then look at question number two. After calming the storm on the lake, Jesus turned to His disciples and asked, 'Where is your faith?'[3] How would you respond if Jesus were to ask you this same question today? What would your answer be? Perhaps, like many people, your faith is in a particular church and you believe membership of that church guarantees your salvation. Or maybe you have put your faith in good works or religious exercises, believing salvation can be earned or merited through participation in such activities. It may be that you are depending upon the prayers and intercession of various Saints for your salvation.

On the other hand, you may be a person who does not even believe in the existence of God. It may interest you to know that regardless of colour, culture or creed, we all have one thing in common – we are all sinners. According to the Scriptures 'there is none righteous, no, not one.[4] For all have sinned, and come short of the glory of God'.[5] This includes people of every religious persuasion and also atheists and agnostics. All are in need of salvation. The apostle Peter made it clear that salvation is found in Christ alone when he said 'Neither is there salvation in any other: for there is none other name under heaven given among men, whereby we must be saved'.[6]

Where is your faith? May the Lord impress upon your heart your need to put your faith in Jesus Christ and to trust (rely on, depend upon) Him for your salvation. May He cause you to act without delay. 'Seek ye the Lord while he may be found, call ye upon him while he is near'.[7] Do not hesitate, for 'now is the accepted time; behold, now is the day of salvation'.[8] Jesus said, 'Behold, I stand at the door, and knock: if any man hear my voice, and open the door, I will come in to him, and will sup with him, and he with me'.[9]

Lesson 1

Background to the Gospel of Luke

Luke Chapter 1

Who was Luke?

Luke, the author of this Gospel, was a medical doctor. The apostle Paul refers to him as 'Luke, the beloved physician'.[1] It is not surprising therefore that, in his writings, Luke makes reference to a number of medical conditions. Among the ailments mentioned by Dr. Luke are deafness, blindness, dropsy, paralysis, leprosy and haemorrhage. Luke presents Jesus as the Great Physician and highlights the fact that He healed all kinds of illnesses and even raised people from the dead.

In the Gospel of Luke the doctor deals with a number of issues, including the following:
(a) A three-day search for a twelve-year-old boy who went missing (Ch.2).
(b) A dead man who sat up and began to speak (Ch.7).
(c) A great robbery (Ch.8).
(d) A herd of pigs which went swimming (Ch.8).
(e) Two religious ministers who refused to help an injured man (Ch.10).
(f) Three loaves of bread borrowed at midnight (Ch.11).
(g) Down and outs who were invited to supper (Ch.14).
(h) A beggar whose sores were licked by dogs (Ch.16).
(i) A woman who was widowed seven times (Ch.20).
(j) Earthquakes, famine and pestilence (Ch.21).
(k) A man who kissed the Saviour and then went to hell (Ch.22).
(l) A murderer freed and an innocent man executed (Ch. 23).
(m) An abandoned Son who died in the darkness (Ch.23).
(n) An empty tomb (Ch.24).
The doctor's letter is an encouragement to self-examination. It highlights the need for an immediate spiritual check-up. It is a prescription for a spiritual tonic that will heal the sin-sick soul. The Lord said, 'I will bring it health and cure, and I will cure them, and will reveal unto them the abundance of peace

and truth.[2] And I will cleanse them from all their iniquity, whereby they have sinned against me; and I will pardon all their iniquities, whereby they have sinned, and whereby they have transgressed against me'.[3]

A Request

Luke, who was a Gentile convert, accompanied the apostle Paul on his second and third missionary journeys. He tells us of a very important event which happened during their travels. When they had arrived at a place called Troas 'a vision appeared to Paul in the night; There stood a man of Macedonia, and prayed him, saying, Come over into Macedonia, and help us. And after he had seen the vision, immediately we endeavoured to go into Macedonia, assuredly gathering that the Lord had called us for to preach the gospel unto them'.[4]

The Response

Paul, Silas, Timothy and Luke responded to God's call and went to Philippi, a city in Macedonia, to preach the gospel. They realised these people were in spiritual darkness and needed help. They were sinners, just like everyone else, 'for *all* have sinned, and come short of the glory of God'.[5] They needed to be converted. Otherwise they would be eternally lost, for 'the wages of sin is death'.[6] Jesus spoke of sinners being 'cast into hell fire'.[7] He said they would be sent 'into everlasting fire, prepared for the devil and his angels'.[8] He made it clear that sinners 'shall go away into everlasting punishment'.[9]

Paul and his friends faithfully proclaimed the gospel in Philippi. Lydia and her household, and also the local jailer and his household, responded to the preaching of the gospel and were converted. These new converts formed the nucleus of the church at Philippi. One of Paul's writings, the Epistle to the Philippians, is addressed to this church.

Your Response

Many of us have heard a lot, from various sources, concerning Christ and Christianity. You now have the opportunity to study the Scriptures, 'which are able to make thee wise unto salvation through faith which is in Christ Jesus'.[10] According to the Scriptures we are all sinners and 'there is none righteous, no, not one'.[11] Some people may think they are not too bad and have not committed any serious sins. However, even liars are in danger of eternal damnation in hell. The apostle John highlights the fact that 'the fearful, and unbelieving, and the abominable, and murderers, and whoremongers, and sorcerers, and idolaters, and all liars, shall have their part in the lake which burneth with fire and brimstone: which is the second death'.[12]

How then can we escape this fearful prospect of spending eternity suffering in the fires of hell? Jesus left us in no doubt concerning what we must do. He said, 'Repent ye, and believe the gospel'.[13] We must:

(a) **Recognise** and acknowledge the fact that we are sinners. 'There is not a just man upon earth, that doeth good, and sinneth not'.[14]

(b) **Confess** our sins to God. 'If we confess our sins, he is faithful and just to forgive us our sins, and to cleanse us from all unrighteousness'.[15]

(c) **Repent** of our sins. Repentance includes not just regret or sorrow for your sins, but also a determination to turn from your sinful way of life and to follow the Lord. 'Except ye repent, ye shall all likewise perish'.[16]

(d) **Respond** to God's offer of forgiveness. 'Come now, and let us reason together, saith the Lord: though your sins be as scarlet, they shall be as white as snow; though they be red like crimson, they shall be as wool'.[17]

(e) **Rely** upon (put our faith in and depend upon) Jesus for our salvation. He took upon Himself the guilt of our sins and paid the penalty for them. By paying the penalty for our sins Jesus secured a pardon for us. This pardon will be put to the account of all who put their faith in Jesus and trust Him as Saviour. 'Let the wicked forsake his way, and the unrighteous man his thoughts: and let him return unto the Lord; and he will have mercy upon him; and to our God, for he will abundantly pardon'.[18]

(f) **Reach** out by faith and receive the gift of eternal life from God. We cannot earn or merit salvation, but Christ purchased our salvation for us when He paid for our sins. He now offers us eternal life as a free gift. 'The gift of God is eternal life through Jesus Christ our Lord'. [19]

Something to Consider

Have you accepted the pardon Jesus purchased for you when He paid the penalty for your sins by dying on the cross at Calvary as your substitute? Have you accepted the free gift of eternal life that God is offering to you? Why not reach out by faith and do so today?

Lesson 2

The Angel visits Mary

Luke Chapter 1

How could this Happen?

A virgin named Mary was pledged to be married to Joseph, the local carpenter. God sent the angel Gabriel to inform Mary that, though she was a virgin, she would conceive and give birth to a son. Mary wondered how this could happen. The angel told her that the conception of the child in her womb would be as a result of the intervention of the Holy Spirit. This young woman did not fully understand the implications of what might happen. However, she realised God had a personal interest in her as an individual, so she was prepared to trust Him concerning what was to come.

What would People Think?

Mary loved Joseph and planned to marry him. But now she was faced with a very difficult situation. How could she tell him that she had conceived a child? How would he respond? What would he think? Would he cancel all the wedding plans? What about her own parents? What would they say? Would they feel she was bringing disgrace upon them and upon the whole family? What about Joseph's parents and family? How would they respond? What about all her friends? What would they think of her now? What about all the neighbours? Wouldn't some people just love to spread gossip and scandal? And what about the Jewish Priests? Would they put her out of the synagogue? Would they classify her as an immoral woman? What about her reputation? Would anybody at all believe her when she told them that she had conceived by the power of the Holy Spirit? None of these things prevented Mary from submitting herself into God's hands and trusting Him for the future. Her unconditional surrender to the Lord is summed up in her own words. She said, 'Behold the handmaid of the Lord; be it unto me according to thy word'.[1]

What about Joseph?

Joseph could trace his ancestry right back to King David. When Mary informed him that she was pregnant, Joseph must have come to the conclusion that she had been unfaithful to him. Consequently, he could not envisage taking her home to live with him in the usual marriage relationship. 'But while he thought on these things, behold, the angel of the Lord appeared unto him in a dream'.[2] Joseph must have been greatly relieved when the angel informed him that it was by the power of the Holy Spirit, and not in the natural way, that Mary had conceived. Any doubts he might have had concerning Mary's faithfulness to him disappeared when he realised that the child who was to be born to her was not the son of a human father. This child was God's own Son. In fact He was Emmanuel, God the Son. When Joseph awoke from his sleep he did as the angel of the Lord had commanded him and took Mary to his home as his wife.

What about you?

Both Mary and Joseph willingly submitted themselves to the Lord's will. And what about you, dear Friend? Perhaps you have been considering submitting your life to God? The Scriptures make it clear that 'if we say that we have no sin, we deceive ourselves.[3] We are all as an unclean thing, and all our righteousnesses are as filthy rags'.[4] We are left in no doubt concerning the fact that as sinners we are all liable to sin's penalty, which consists of both physical and spiritual death (separation from God for all eternity). The apostle Paul tells us that 'by one man sin entered into the world, and death by sin; and so death passed upon all men, for that all have sinned'.[5] John highlights the fact that all who die in their sins 'shall have their part in the lake which burneth with fire and brimstone: which is the second death'.[6]

Church membership, sacraments and involvement in good works or religious activities cannot save sinners. According to the Scriptures salvation is found in Christ alone. When Thomas questioned the Saviour, Jesus said to him, 'I am the way, the truth, and the life: no man cometh unto the Father, but by me'.[7] On another occasion Jesus said, 'He that heareth my word, and believeth on him that sent me, hath everlasting life, and shall not come into condemnation; but is passed from death unto life'.[8]

Two More Questions

'How can ye escape the damnation of hell?'[9]
'How shall we escape if we neglect so great salvation?'[10]

What will People Say?

Friend, you now know that in order to be saved you need to 'repent...and be converted, that your sins may be blotted out'.[11] Yet you are hesitating! Perhaps you are worried about what your family, friends, neighbours or clergy might say if you put your faith in Christ and depend upon Him alone for your salvation? However, there is no need to fear, for the Lord has given a wonderful promise to all who will trust Him as Saviour. He said, 'I will never leave thee, nor forsake thee'.[12] So we can say, 'The Lord is my helper, and I will not fear what man shall do unto me'.[13]

Something to Consider

Why not take the Lord at His promise and trust Him to save your soul and to give you the strength to live the Christian life?

Lesson 3

The Conception of Jesus

Luke Chapter 1

The conception of the child in Mary's womb would be a unique event. Such a thing had never happened before and would never happen again.

It would be a Miraculous Conception

It would be by the power of the Holy Ghost, and not in the natural way, that Mary would conceive. When the angel Gabriel appeared to her he said, 'The Holy Ghost shall come upon thee, and the power of the Highest shall overshadow thee: therefore also that holy thing [child] which shall be born of thee shall be called the Son of God'.[1]

It would be an Immaculate Conception

God the Son, having a Divine nature, was about to assume, or take upon Himself human nature. But this human nature was very different from the nature of everyone else in that it was untainted by sin. According to the Scriptures Jesus was the **only** one ever born of a woman who could be called the Holy One. Unlike everyone else, He had not inherited the sinful nature which Adam passed on to all his descendants.

The author of the book of Hebrews makes it clear that Jesus is our high priest. This high priest of ours is 'holy, harmless [blameless], undefiled, separate from sinners, and made higher than the heavens'.[2] He understands our weaknesses because He Himself was tempted. 'We have not an high priest which cannot be touched with the feeling of our infirmities; but was in all points tempted like as we are, yet **without sin**'.[3] Peter described Jesus as 'a lamb without blemish and without spot.[4] Who did no sin, neither was guile found in his mouth: Who, when he was reviled, reviled not again; when he suffered, he threatened not: but committed himself to him that judgeth righteously'.[5]

The prophet Isaiah, writing over 700 years before the birth of Christ, reminds us that 'He [Jesus] was oppressed, and he was afflicted, yet he opened not his mouth: he is brought as a lamb to the slaughter, and as a sheep before her shearers is dumb, so he openeth not his mouth'.[6] John the Baptist identified Jesus as 'the Lamb of God, which taketh away the sin of the world'.[7] The apostle John reminds us of why the Lamb of God came into the world. He tells us that 'He was manifested to take away our sins; and in him is no sin'.[8] Jesus would offer Himself in sacrifice as a substitute for sinners. He would bear the penalty for their sins by suffering and dying on their behalf. To be an acceptable and effective substitute it was necessary that He Himself be perfectly holy.

This Child had Two Natures

He had a Divine nature. In the Gospel of Luke Jesus is described as 'the Son of the Highest' and 'the Son of God'.[9] In Matthew's Gospel Jesus is called 'Emmanuel, which being interpreted is, God with us'.[10] An Old Testament prophecy concerning Jesus tells us that 'his name shall be called Wonderful, Counsellor, The mighty God, The everlasting Father, The Prince of Peace'.[11]

He also shared in human nature. 'But when the fullness of the time was come, God sent forth his Son, made of a woman, made under the law, To redeem them that were under the law, that we might receive the adoption of sons.[12] And the Word was made flesh, and dwelt among us, (and we beheld his glory, the glory as of the only begotten of the Father,) full of grace and truth'.[13] Jesus is one in nature with the Father and the Holy Spirit, 'but made himself of no reputation, and took upon him the form of a servant, and was made in the likeness of men: And being found in fashion as a man, he humbled himself, and became obedient unto death, even the death of the cross'.[14]

The Only One

According to the Scriptures Jesus was the **only** child who was conceived without sin. In other words He was the **only** child who did not inherit a sinful nature. He is the **only** One who has lived on earth of whom it could be said that He never, in any way, did wrong. For our salvation it was necessary that the Saviour be God, human and sinless. Jesus Christ alone is all three and, as such, is the perfect and only Saviour.

Something to Consider

Salvation is found in Christ alone. 'Neither is there salvation in any other: for there is none other name under heaven given among men, whereby we must be saved'.[15] Have you asked Christ to be your Saviour? Why not ask Him today?

Lesson 4

The Birth of Jesus

Luke Chapter 2

At the Right Time

Caesar Augustus, ruler of the pagan Roman Empire, issued the command that a census should be taken (v. 1). He had no idea that God would actually use this decree for the fulfilment of His purposes concerning the salvation of His people. The prophet Micah, who lived over 700 years before the birth of Christ, identified Bethlehem as the birthplace of the Messiah. This census was called at just the right time to ensure that Joseph and Mary would be in that very city when the time arrived for the birth of the child. The apostle Paul reminds us that 'when the fullness of the time was come, God sent forth His Son, made of a woman, made under the law, To redeem them that were under the law, that we might receive the adoption of sons'.[1]

No Room in the Inn

When Joseph and Mary arrived in Bethlehem it was already overcrowded and all of the available accommodation was occupied. They must have been very disappointed when they were told that 'there was no room for them in the inn'.[2] Little did the owner of the inn realise that he was refusing entry not only to Joseph and Mary, but also to the Saviour.

Mary gave birth to her firstborn son in a stable. She wrapped him in swaddling clothes and laid Him in a manger, a feeding trough for animals. God the Son left the splendour of heaven and took upon Himself human nature. The birth of the Messiah took place not in a royal palace, but in a lowly stable. He humbled Himself for our sakes. 'Ye know the grace of our Lord Jesus Christ, that, though he was rich, yet for your sakes he became poor, that ye through his poverty might be rich'.[3]

Do you have Room?

There was no room in the inn for the Saviour. There are many people today whose hearts are so full of plans, aspirations and lust for pleasures, riches and other things, that there is no room for the Saviour.

Dear Friend, let me ask you a question! What would you do if the Saviour knocked on your door today, seeking admission? You will probably answer this question by saying you would invite Him in! But let me ask you another question! How have you responded to the fact that for some time now the Lord has been knocking on the door of your heart (the door of your life) seeking admission? Jesus said, 'Behold, I stand at the door, and knock: if any man hear my voice, and open the door, I will come in to him, and will sup with him, and he with me'.[4]

Many believe that Jesus entered their heart as a result of some childhood ritual, church ordinance or sacrament. However, the Scriptures make it very clear that He stands outside of our lives and will enter by invitation only. Jesus knocks and gives us the opportunity to invite Him in. He will not force His way into anyone's life, but will gladly come in if invited. He promises to come in as Saviour and Lord if we ask Him. Have you invited Him in?

Will He knock Again?

Perhaps you feel your life is full right now and there is no room in it for Jesus. Maybe you have decided that you will consider allowing Him in eventually. But you have no intention of doing this until you have enjoyed life to the full. Friend, how do you know Jesus will continue knocking on your heart? Did you know that the Lord has said, 'My Spirit shall not always strive with man?'[5] What makes you think He will knock again tomorrow if you refuse Him entry today? How do you know you will have the opportunity to invite Him in tomorrow?

Will you have Time?

We all knew people who died suddenly. What if this were to happen to you today? Are you sure you would go to heaven? Do you think the Lord will allow you into heaven if you refuse to allow Him into your life? Perhaps you will be so busy tomorrow that you will not have time to even consider the matter. None of us know what family crisis or urgent business matters may arise tomorrow that will demand our full attention. So don't delay! 'Today if ye will hear his voice, harden not your hearts'.[6]

Something to Consider

In his first Epistle, the apostle John reminds us that 'God hath given to us eternal life, and this life is in his Son. He that hath the Son hath life; and he that hath not the Son of God hath not life'.[7] Do you have Jesus in your life? Have you invited Him in as Saviour? If not, may I urge you to invite Him in today.

Lesson 5

The Child Jesus in the Temple

Luke Chapter 2

'Thou shalt call His Name Jesus'

When the Child Jesus was eight days old Joseph and Mary brought Him to the temple to be circumcised. Both Mary and Joseph had been instructed by the angel concerning the child's name. When the angel explained to Joseph about the conception of the child in Mary's womb he left him in no doubt concerning who the child was, what His name should be and the purpose of His birth. He said, 'She shall bring forth a son, and thou shalt call his name JESUS: for he shall save his people from their sins'.[1] The Son of God came into the world for a very specific purpose, which is clearly stated in the words, 'He shall save his people from their sins'.

Forty days after the birth of the baby, Mary and Joseph brought Him to the Temple in Jerusalem for the purification service and also to present Him to the Lord. They were fulfilling God's instructions which are outlined in the Old Testament. Though Mary had given birth to God's Son she did not see herself as being different from any other mother. She, too, was subject to God and to His Law, and made the required sacrifices and offerings.

Simeon sees the Saviour

While Joseph, Mary and the infant Jesus were in the Temple they met Simeon. He was one of the many people who were looking forward to the coming of the Saviour. The birth of the Saviour had been foretold by the prophet Isaiah who said, 'The Lord himself shall give you a sign; Behold, a virgin shall conceive, and bear a son, and shall call his name Immanuel.[2] For unto us a child is born, unto us a son is given: and the government shall be upon his shoulder: and his name shall be called Wonderful, Counsellor, The mighty God, The everlasting Father, The Prince of Peace. Of the increase of his government and peace there shall be no end, upon the throne of David, and upon his kingdom, to order it, and to establish it with judgment and with justice from henceforth even for ever. The zeal of the Lord of hosts will perform this'.[3]

The Holy Spirit revealed to Simeon that this Child was 'The Lord's Christ'. He was the Anointed One, the Messiah. God had promised this righteous man that before he died he would see the Messiah (Luke Ch.2 v. 26). Simeon realised that the child he held in his arms was the One through whom God would save His people. He knew that salvation was not in a religious system, but in the Lord Jesus Christ. Many years later the apostle John, in his first Letter, explains that salvation is found in Christ alone. He tells us that 'God hath given to us eternal life, and this life is in His Son'.[4]

Planned, Prepared and Provided

Simeon gave thanks to God and said, 'Mine eyes have seen thy salvation, Which thou hast prepared before the face of all people'.[5] Our salvation was planned, prepared and provided by God. It is not a human achievement. It is a Divine gift. The apostle Paul explains that 'the wages of sin is death; but the gift of God is eternal life through Jesus Christ our Lord'.[6]

All people, both Jews and Gentiles (the world outside of Israel), need to be saved from sin's penalty. Now the One of whom the prophets had spoken had arrived, 'to open the blind eyes, to bring out the prisoners from the prison, and them that sit in darkness out of the prison house'.[7] The Saviour had now appeared on the scene of time, to fulfil God's eternal purposes to redeem His people. The Scriptures make it clear that 'Christ Jesus came into the world to save sinners'.[8]

Have you Heard?

The message of salvation through faith in Jesus Christ is for all people. Jesus said to His disciples, 'Go ye into all the world, and preach the gospel to every creature'.[9] The apostle Paul was motivated by the fact that the Lord had said, 'I have set thee to be a light of the Gentiles, that thou shouldest be for salvation unto the ends of the earth.'[10]

The words of one of the songs sung in heaven remind us that, as a result of the preaching of the gospel, people from all over the world will be converted. The singers worshipped Jesus as they sang a new song, saying, 'Thou are worthy to take the book, and to open the seals thereof: for thou wast slain, and hast redeemed us to God by thy blood out of every kindred, and tongue, and people, and nation'.[11] The Child whom Simeon held in his arms was the One whose life, death and resurrection from the grave would make it possible for sinners to be saved.

Something to Consider

On the cross Jesus took the place of sinners and paid the penalty for their sins. All who repent of their sins and put their faith in Him will be saved. Have you put your faith in the Lord Jesus Christ? Are you depending upon Him for your salvation? Instead of looking to religion or looking to your own good works to save you, look to the Lord, who said, 'Look unto me, and be ye saved, all the ends of the earth; for I am God, and there is none else'.[12]

Lesson 6

Christ is Greater than the Prophets and Angels

Luke Chapters 3 and 4

Jesus is Greater than the Prophets

This is an issue of great importance, for we live in days when Muslims claim that Jesus was no more than a prophet and would count Mohammed as being worthy of the same honour as our Saviour. Many Jews also believe Jesus was only a prophet and would certainly refuse to acknowledge Him as being greater than Moses. However, the Scriptures specifically testify to the pre-eminence of Christ. We are left in no doubt concerning the fact that 'this man [Jesus] was counted worthy of more glory than Moses'.[1]

The Scriptures make it clear that Jesus was greater than John the Baptist (Please read Luke Ch.3 v. 16 and Matthew Ch.3 v. 11). The fact that Christ is greater than the prophets is clearly established by the fact that 'God, who at sundry times and in divers manners spake in time past unto the fathers by the prophets, Hath in these last days spoken unto us by his Son, whom he hath appointed heir of all things, by whom also he made the worlds; Who being the brightness of his glory, and the express image of his person, and upholding all things by the word of his power, when he had by himself purged our sins, sat down on the right hand of the majesty on high'.[2]

Christ and Creation

Jehovah's Witnesses claim that Jesus was no more than a created being. However, the Scriptures make it perfectly clear that Jesus was not created but was, in fact, active in creation. '**All** things were made by him; and without him was not any thing made that was made.[3] For by him were all things created, that are in heaven, and that are in earth, visible and invisible, whether they be thrones, or dominions, or principalities, or powers: all things were created by him, and for him: And he is before all things, and by him all things consist.⁴ God...hath in these last days spoken unto us by his Son, whom he hath appointed heir of all things, by whom also he made the worlds; Who being the brightness of his glory, and the express image of his person, and upholding all things by the word of his power, when he had by himself purged our sins, sat down on the right hand of the Majesty on high'.⁵

Jesus is Greater than the Angels

Jehovah's Witnesses also claim that Jesus was only an angel. But Christ's superiority over the angels is outlined very clearly in the Scriptures. When Jesus ascended to heaven He sat down at the right hand of His Father, 'being made so much better than the angels, as he hath by inheritance obtained a more excellent name than they. For unto which of the angels said he at any time, Thou art my Son, this day have I begotten thee? And again, I will be to him a Father, and he shall be to me a Son? And again, when he bringeth in the firstbegotten into the world, he saith, And let all the angels of God worship him...But unto the Son he saith, Thy throne O God, is for ever and ever...And Thou, Lord, in the beginning hast laid the foundation of the earth; and the heavens are the works of thine hands...But to which of the angels said he at any time, Sit on my right hand, until I make thine enemies thy footstool?'⁶

Christ the Giver of Spiritual Life

John the Baptist was convinced that he was unworthy to even untie the sandals of Jesus. He drew a contrast between what he himself was doing and what Jesus would do. John would baptise with water, the outward symbol of cleansing, but Christ would baptise with the Holy Spirit, effecting an inward cleansing, a cleansing of the heart. Jesus would bestow the Spirit of Regeneration, causing people to be born again (born from above). When He spoke to Nicodemus, a religious leader and teacher, Jesus highlighted people's need of the regenerating Spirit. He said, 'Verily, verily, I say unto thee, Except a man be born again, he cannot see the kingdom of God.⁷ Except a man be born of water and of the Spirit, he cannot enter into the kingdom of God. That which is born of the flesh is flesh; and that which is born of the Spirit is spirit. Marvel not that I said unto thee, Ye must be born again'.[8] Jesus was pointing out to Nicodemus the fact that humans can only reproduce human life, but the Holy Spirit gives new life from heaven.

The apostle Paul testifies to the fact that a sinner cannot be saved apart from the regenerating work of the Holy Spirit. He reminds us that it is 'not by works of righteousness which we have done, but according to his mercy he saved us, by the washing of regeneration, and renewing of the Holy Ghost; Which he shed on us abundantly through Jesus Christ our Saviour'.[9] This regenerating Spirit would, like fire, purify the person by removing the pollution from the heart.

He alone can meet Your Need

John the Baptist could not cleanse a person's heart. Neither could Moses or any of the prophets. Even an angel could not do it. John pointed to Jesus and said, 'He shall baptize you with the Holy Ghost, and with fire'.[10] Christ alone can meet the sinner's need. 'Neither is there salvation in any other: for there is none other name under heaven given among men, whereby we must be saved'.[11] Christ alone can meet your need! The apostle John reminds us that 'God hath given to us eternal life, and this life is in his Son'.[12]

Something to Consider

The Lord said, 'Call unto me, and I will answer thee'.[13]
Why not call upon the Lord today? If you sincerely repent of your sins and ask Him to save your soul, He will.

Lesson 7

The Saviour Identifies with Sinners

Luke Chapter 3

The Sinless Saviour

Christ Himself was sinless. The apostle John highlights this when he tells us that 'He was manifested to take away our sins; and in him is no sin'.[1] Peter makes it clear that we are redeemed 'with the precious blood of Christ, as of a lamb without blemish and without spot.[2] Who did no sin, neither was guile found in his mouth'.[3] Christ is identified in the Scriptures as our sinless high priest. The author of the book of Hebrews reminds us that 'we have not an high priest which cannot be touched with the feeling of our infirmities; but was in all points tempted like as we are, yet without sin.[4] For such an high priest became us, who is holy, harmless [blameless], undefiled, separate from sinners, and made higher than the heavens'.[5]

The Sinless Substitute

Though Jesus had no sin in Him, yet we read in the Scriptures that He took the guilt of people's sin upon Himself and bore its punishment on behalf of others. The fact that Jesus would become a substitute for sinners is revealed in many of the Old Testament prophecies. When Isaiah prophesied about Christ he said, 'Surely he hath borne our griefs, and carried our sorrows: yet we did esteem him stricken, smitten of God, and afflicted. But he was wounded for our transgressions, he was bruised for our iniquities: the chastisement of our peace was upon him; and with his stripes we are healed. All we like sheep have gone astray; we have turned every one to his own way; and the Lord hath laid on him the iniquity of us all'.[6]

Love Publicly Demonstrated

We see Christ, the Sinless One, humbly submitting Himself to baptism, which was an outward sign symbolising the cleansing of sin. This was a public affirmation of Jesus' willingness to take upon Himself the sins of others. These sins could not be cleansed by the waters of baptism, but would be dealt with at Calvary. There was nothing we could do to save ourselves, 'but God commendeth his love toward us, in that, while we were yet sinners, Christ died for us'.[7] God publicly demonstrated His love for us as Jesus suffered and died upon the cross as our substitute.

The Saviour Publicly Identified

As soon as Jesus was baptised the Holy Spirit descended on Him. John the Baptist said, 'I saw the Spirit descending from heaven like a dove, and it abode upon him'.[8] The Father's voice of love and approval was heard from heaven as He, too, publicly identified the Messiah. He said, 'This is my beloved Son, in whom I am well pleased'.[9] On this historic day, as Jesus publicly assumed His work as Messiah, we see the Trinity (God the Father, God the Son and God the Holy Ghost) demonstrating the fact that in the work of salvation the three are one. It left John the Baptist in no doubt concerning the identity of the Saviour. Speaking of Jesus, he said, 'I saw, and bear record that this is the Son of God'.[10]

The Saviour Associates with Sinners

The fact that Jesus even associated with sinners was often questioned by his critics. Matthew tells us that on one occasion 'as Jesus sat at meat in the house, behold, many publicans and sinners came and sat down with him and his disciples. And when the Pharisees saw it, they said to his disciples, Why eateth your Master with publicans and sinners?'[11] Jesus responded by saying, 'I am not come to call the righteous, but sinners to repentance'.[12] Luke writes of a sinful woman who washed Jesus' feet with her tears. Jesus said, 'Her sins, which are many, are forgiven'.[13] He also highlights the fact that Jesus welcomes repentant sinners. One day 'there drew near unto him all the publicans and sinners for to hear him. And the Pharisees and scribes murmured, saying, This man receiveth [welcomes] sinners, and eateth with them'.[14]

Will You Come Now?

Throughout His ministry Jesus made it very clear that He had come to rescue sinners. He said, 'The Son of man is come to seek and to save that which was lost'.[15] This means that there is hope for the vilest of sinners. Regardless of how serious our sin is, was can receive forgiveness if we come to the Saviour in sincere repentance. 'Come now, and let us reason together, saith the Lord: though your sins be as scarlet, they shall be as white as snow; though they be red like crimson, they shall be as wool'.[16] The repentant sinner who comes to the Lord seeking forgiveness will not be turned away. Jesus said, 'Him that cometh to me I will in no wise cast out'.[17]

Something to Consider

Have you come to the Lord in sincere repentance for your sins, determined to turn away from your sinful way of life? Have you come to Him in faith, believing He bore the penalty for your sins by suffering and dying on the cross in your place? Are you trusting in Him for your salvation? Are you depending upon Him to save your soul? In Luke Ch.15 v. 2 we are told that Jesus welcomes sinners. Friend, He will welcome you, forgive your sins and save your soul if you come to Him today.

Lesson 8

Jesus Shows His Power

Luke Chapter 4

Throughout His ministry, Jesus manifested His Divine Power (His Omnipotence). His power was displayed in the following ways:

Power over the Devil

In Luke Ch.4 vs. 1 - 14 we read of how Jesus, after forty days of fasting in the wilderness, returned victoriously, in the power of the Spirit, having defeated the devil's attempts to make Him sin.

Power over the Demons

In Luke Ch.4 vs. 33 - 36 we see Jesus' power and authority manifested over the demons. The demons acknowledged who Jesus was, saying, 'I know thee who thou art; the Holy One of God'.[1] The people who were present and witnessed what had happened were amazed and remarked that 'with authority and power he commandeth the unclean spirits and they come out'.[2] [Please read Luke Ch.9 vs. 37 – 42].

Power over Sickness

After Jesus had healed a man who was afflicted with leprosy, crowds of people came to hear Him and to be healed of their sicknesses. Details of this incident are recorded in Luke Ch.5 vs. 12 – 15. Further examples of Jesus' power over sickness can be found in Luke Ch.8 vs. 43 - 48; Ch.13 vs. 10 – 13 and Ch.18 vs. 35 – 43.

Power over Death

On a number of occasions Jesus publicly demonstrated His power over death. In Luke Ch.7 vs. 11 – 16 we read of the occasion on which He raised the widow's son from the dead. The account of how Jesus brought the daughter of Jairus back to life can be found in Luke Ch.8 vs. 49 – 56. Jesus went to the tomb of Lazarus, who had been dead for four days, and 'cried with a loud voice, Lazarus, come forth. And he that was dead came forth'.[3] In Luke Ch.24 we read of how Christ's power over death was ultimately demonstrated by His own resurrection from the dead. The apostle John records the words of Jesus, who said, 'I lay down my life, that I might take it again. No man taketh it from me, but I lay it down of myself. I have power to lay it down, and I have power to take it again.[4] I am he that liveth, and was dead; and, behold, I am alive for evermore'.[5]

Power over Nature

Jesus controlled the shoal of fish. We read of this in Luke Ch.5 vs. 1 – 9.

Jesus stilled the tempest. Luke records this account in Ch.8 vs. 22 – 25. Jesus rebuked the wind and the waves, causing the storm to cease. His disciples, amazed at what they witnessed, asked, 'What manner of man is this! for he commandeth even the winds and water, and they obey him'.[6]

Jesus performed the miracle of the loaves and fish. This is found in Luke Ch.9 vs. 10 - 17.

Jesus walked on the water. Matthew tells us about this occasion. Shortly after performing the miracle of multiplying the loaves and fish, 'Jesus constrained his disciples to get into a ship, and to go before him unto the other side, while he sent the multitudes away. And when he had sent the multitudes away, he went up into a mountain apart to pray: and when the evening was come, he was there alone. But the ship was now in the midst of the sea, tossed with waves: for the wind was contrary. And in the fourth watch of the night Jesus went unto them, walking on the sea'.[7]

Jesus turned water into wine. In the Gospel of John we read of this very first miracle which Jesus performed. John writes: 'There was a marriage in Cana of Galilee; and the mother of Jesus was there: And both Jesus was called, and his disciples, to the marriage. And when they wanted wine, the mother of Jesus saith unto him, They have no wine…Jesus saith unto them, Fill the waterpots with water. And they filled them up to the brim. And he saith unto them, Draw out now, and bear unto the governor of the feast. And they bare it. When the ruler of the feast had tasted the water that was made wine, and knew not whence it was: (but the servants which drew the water knew;) the governor of the feast called the bridegroom, And saith unto him, Every man at the beginning doth set forth good wine; and when men have well drunk, then that which is worse: but thou hast kept the good wine until now. This beginning of miracles did Jesus in Cana of Galilee, and manifested forth his glory; and his disciples believed on him'.[8]

Power to Forgive Sins

'Who can forgive sins, but God alone?'[9] In Luke Ch.5 vs. 18 – 26 Jesus' power to forgive sins is publicly demonstrated. Some men brought their paralysed friend to Jesus. When the Saviour saw their faith He said to the man afflicted with palsy, 'Thy sins are forgiven thee'. The scribes and the Pharisees began to question what Jesus said, and asked, 'Who is this which speaketh blasphemies? Who can forgive sins, but God alone?' They were correct in ascribing the power to forgive sins to God alone. None of the prophets or priests had this power. By saying that He forgave sins Jesus was understood to be proclaiming that He was Divine. The Lord then provided further proof of His power and authority by performing a miracle. All who witnessed it would have to admit that the power of God was required to perform such a miracle. Turning to the Scribes and the Pharisees, Jesus asked if it was easier to say, 'Thy sins are forgiven thee', or to say, 'Rise up and walk'. To prove to them that He had power on earth to forgive sins, He said to the man who was paralysed, 'Arise, and take up thy couch, and go into thine house'. The man immediately stood up, picked up his bed and walked home. Jesus, God the Son manifest in the flesh, clearly demonstrated the fact that He not only had power to heal physical infirmities, but also to forgive sins.

Left in No Doubt

These accounts of the manifestation of Jesus' Power (His Omnipotence) are recorded in the Scriptures so that we may be left in no doubt concerning the fact that 'God hath visited his people'[10] in the Person of the Lord Jesus Christ.

Something to Consider

If we refuse to accept the fact that we are sinners and if we continue to live in denial of this truth, then we delude ourselves. The Scriptures make it clear that 'if we say that we have no sin, we deceive ourselves, and the truth is not in us'.[11] In fact, 'if we say we have not sinned, we make him [God] a liar'.[12] By refusing to accept that what God says about us is true, we are declaring Him to be a liar. However, if we admit that we are sinners and 'if we confess our sins [to God], he is faithful and just to forgive us our sins, and to cleanse us from all unrighteousness'.[13]

Have you acknowledged the fact that you are a sinner? Have you confessed your sins to the Lord and asked Him to forgive, cleanse and save you? Why not do it right now?

Lesson 9

Christ's Mission

God the Son left the splendour of heaven and came to earth, taking upon Himself human nature. The purpose of His Incarnation was announced by an angel who appeared to Joseph in a dream. He said, 'Joseph, thou son of David, fear not to take unto thee Mary thy wife: for that which is conceived in her is of the Holy Ghost. And she shall bring forth a son, and thou shalt call his name JESUS: for he shall save his people from their sins'.[1]

Throughout His ministry Jesus left the following people in no doubt concerning the work He had come to do:

A Tax Collector

Zacchaeus was a tax collector. He was a small man and could not see Jesus because of the large crowd which had gathered around. So he climbed up into a tree. Jesus looked up, saw him and told him to come down. He then explained to Zacchaeus that 'the Son of man is come to seek and to save that which was lost'.[2]

A Ruler of the Jews

Nicodemus was a Pharisee, a member of the Jewish Ruling Council and a teacher of the Law. As He explained the way of salvation to Nicodemus, Jesus told him that He had not come to reject sinners but to save them. He told him that 'God sent not His Son into the world to condemn the world; but that the world through him might be saved'.[3]

The Jews

Many of the Jews still refused to recognise Jesus as Saviour, even after witnessing His miracles. Some of those who did believe in Him were afraid that if they confessed their faith in Christ openly, the Pharisees would put them out of the synagogue. Jesus told them that He had come as a light into the world, so that anyone who put their faith (trust) in Him and relied upon Him for their salvation would no longer live in spiritual darkness. He said to them, 'I came not to judge the world, but to save the world'.[4]

The Apostles

On the way to Jerusalem, where He would later be crucified, Jesus explained to His twelve apostles the purpose of His life and death. He said, 'The Son of man came not to be ministered unto, but to minister, and to give his life a ransom for many'.[5]

The Religious Leaders

In John Ch.9 we are told that a man whom Jesus had cured of blindness was thrown out of the synagogue by the Pharisees. The Lord had restored sight to this man's eyes. However, Christ did something far greater than this, for He also cured the man of spiritual blindness. Jesus said, 'As long as I am in the world, I am the light of the world'.[6] As sinners, we are all afflicted with spiritual blindness. The apostle Paul reminds us of the seriousness of this spiritual blindness, and endeavours to impress upon us the need to repent and believe the gospel. He writes, 'If our gospel be hid, it is hid to them that are lost: In whom the god of this world hath blinded the minds of them which believe not, lest the light of the glorious gospel of Christ, who is the image of God, should shine unto them'.[7] Christ alone can dispel the spiritual darkness.

His Disciples

In the Sermon on the Mount Jesus taught His disciples a very important lesson concerning His mission. He said, 'Think not that I am come to destroy the law, or the prophets: I am not come to destroy, but to fulfil'.[8]

Pontius Pilate

While on trial for His life, Jesus explained to Pilate why He had left heaven and taken upon Himself human nature. He said, 'For this cause came I into the world, that I should bear witness unto the truth'.[9]

The People of Capernaum

The preaching of the gospel was a vital part of the work Jesus did. On a particular occasion some people wanted Him to remain with them, but Jesus said, 'I must preach the kingdom of God to other cities also: for therefore am I sent'.[10]

Why He Came

It is vital that we understand why Jesus came into the world. The Scriptures clearly teach that He had a very specific mission to accomplish. The apostle Paul summed it up very well in his letter to Timothy. He said, 'Christ Jesus came into the world to save sinners'.[11] Paul was depending upon Christ for his salvation. The apostle emphasised this very specifically when he referred to Jesus as 'the Son of God, who loved me, and gave himself for me'.[12]

Did You Know?

Did you know that Jesus loves you and gave Himself for you? He loves you so much that He bore the punishment your sins deserved. When He died on the cross as your substitute he purchased for you a Pardon for your sins, Peace with God and a Place in heaven.

Something to Consider

Eternal Life can be yours if you:
(a) Repent of your sins. This means genuine sorrow for your sins and a resolve to turn your back on your sinful way of life.
(b) Put your faith in the Lord Jesus Christ. Put your trust in Him and depend upon Him to save your soul.

Lesson 10

The Parables of Jesus

Luke Chapter 15

Jesus was a great teacher because He told the greatest truths man has ever heard by means of simple village stories which all could understand. Stories about farmers, travellers, servants, sheep, beggars, bread and various subjects held the people's attention as Jesus applied spiritual truths to His hearers.

Luke records the following Parables

The moneylender (Ch.7 vs. 41 – 43)
The sower (Ch.8 vs. 5 – 8, 11- 15)
A lamp under a bowl (Ch.8 v. 16; Ch.11 v. 33)
The good Samaritan (Ch.10 vs. 30 – 37)
A friend in need (Ch.11 vs. 5 – 8)
The rich fool (Ch.12 vs. 16 – 21)
The watchful servants (Ch.12 vs. 35 – 40)
The faithful and wise servants (Ch.12 vs. 42 – 48)
The unfruitful fig tree (Ch.13 vs. 6 – 9)
A mustard seed (Ch.13 vs. 18, 19)
The yeast (Ch.13 vs. 20, 21)
The lowest seat at the feast (Ch.14 vs. 7 – 14)
The great banquet (Ch.14 vs. 16 – 24)
The cost of discipleship (Ch.14 vs. 28 – 33)
The lost sheep (Ch.15 vs. 4 – 7)
The lost coin (Ch.15 vs. 8 – 10)
The prodigal son (Ch.15 vs. 11 – 32)
The shrewd manager (Ch.16 vs. 1 – 8)
The rich man and Lazarus (Ch.16 vs. 19 – 31)
The master and his servant (Ch.17 vs. 7 – 10)
The persistent widow (Ch.18 vs. 2 – 8)
The Pharisee and the tax collector (Ch.18 vs. 10 – 14)

The talents (Ch.19 vs. 12 – 27)
The tenants (Ch.20 vs. 9 – 18)
The fig tree (Ch.21 vs. 29 – 31)

In Luke Ch.15 Jesus tells three parables. He concludes the parable of the lost sheep by saying that there will be joy in heaven over one sinner who repents (v. 7). He ends the parable of the lost coin by reminding those who were listening that 'there is joy in the presence of the angels of God over one sinner that repenteth'.[1]

The Prodigal Son

To emphasise the great value God places on one individual who repents, Jesus told them the parable of the prodigal son. This young man, enticed by the prospect of what the world had to offer, demanded his inheritance and then left home. He squandered his money and eventually found himself destitute. The turning point in his life arrived when 'he came to himself' (v. 17). In other words, the young man came to his senses and realised the seriousness of the condition he was in. He decided he would return to his father. He would confess to his father that he had sinned against him and would seek his forgiveness.

His father saw him returning and ran to meet him. He had compassion on him and welcomed him with open arms. The son confessed to his father that he had sinned against him and was not worthy to be accepted into the family. The loving father forgave him and rejoiced that his wayward son had returned.

The Turning Point

The Scriptures make it clear that 'all have sinned, and come short of the glory of God'.[2] So 'who can say, I have made my heart clean, I am pure from my sin?'[3] None of us can, for 'there is none righteous, no, not one'.[4] We are just like the prodigal son. We want to go our own way. In fact, 'all we like sheep have gone astray; we have turned everyone to his own way'.[5] We are inclined to walk away from the authority and instruction of God the

Father and abandon the Biblical principles we learned from our parents, teachers and religious leaders. The lure of the things of the world attract us and draw us away. Countless men and women who went astray soon discovered that misery and misfortune were all that the world had to offer.

However, many can testify to the fact that the turning point came in their lives when they came to their senses and realised they had turned their backs on God and had walked away from Him. Longing to be delivered and set free from the grip of sin and its consequences, they decided to:
(a) Turn from their waywardness and seek the Lord.
(b) Acknowledge the fact that they were not worthy to be accepted into the Father's family.
(c) Confess to the Father that they had sinned against Him.
(d) Ask the Father to forgive them.

They repented of their sins, determined to change their ways.
The importance of repentance is highlighted by Jesus, who said, 'Except ye repent, ye shall all likewise perish'.[6]

When they came to God they were not turned away.
The Lord said, 'Him that cometh to me I will in no wise cast out'.[7]

When they stopped trying to cover up or hide their sins, but confessed them to God, they were forgiven.
'I acknowledge my sin unto thee, and mine iniquity have I not hid. I said, I will confess my transgressions unto the Lord; and thou forgavest the iniquity of my sin.[8] If we confess our sins, he is faithful and just to forgive us our sins, and to cleanse us from all unrighteousness'.[9]

The Forgiving Father

Our Heavenly Father encourages wayward sinners to return to Him and assures them that if they do so they will be forgiven. He lovingly says, 'Though your sins be as scarlet, they shall be as white as snow; though they be red like crimson, they shall be as wool'.[10] His willingness to pardon the vilest and most wicked sinner is very evident when He says, 'Let the wicked forsake his way, and the unrighteous man his thoughts; and let him return unto the Lord; and he will have mercy upon him; and to our God, for he will abundantly pardon'.[11] The Psalmist reminds us that 'The Lord is merciful and gracious, slow to anger, and plenteous in mercy. He will not always chide: neither will he keep his anger for ever. He hath not dealt with us after our sins; nor rewarded us according to our iniquities. For as the heaven is high above the earth, so great is his mercy toward them that fear him. As far as the east is from the west, so far hath he removed our transgressions from us. Like as a father pitieth his children, so the Lord pitieth them that fear him'.[12]

Lost and Found

In the parable of the prodigal son the father said that his wayward son had been lost, but was now found (vs. 24, 32). It is not God's desire that any of us should be lost. He is 'not willing that any should perish, but that all should come to repentance'.[13] Jesus went to Calvary and paid the penalty for our sins so that we could be saved. He said He had come 'to seek and to save that which was lost'.[14]

No Delay

When the prodigal son came to his senses he immediately got up and went to his father. He did not delay. We should make no delay in seeking God's forgiveness. We should not presume that we have plenty of time left and that we can come to him at a later date. The prophet Isaiah highlights this when he says, 'Seek ye the Lord while he may be found, call ye upon him while he is near'.[15] The apostle Paul seeks to impress upon us the need to treat the matter with a degree of urgency by reminding us that 'now is the accepted time; behold, now is the day of salvation'.[16]

Something to Consider

Why not seek the Lord today? He said, 'Ye shall seek me, and find me, when ye shall search for me with all your heart'.[17] This can be the day of salvation for you if you repent of your sins and put your faith in the Lord Jesus Christ, believing He paid for your sins when He died on the cross at Calvary.

Lesson 11

Jesus is Forsaken

Luke Chapter 23

Forsaken by Others

'He is despised and rejected of men; a man of sorrows, and acquainted with grief'.[1]   Over 700 years before Christ was crucified the prophet Isaiah described Him as One who would be forsaken. By examining the Gospels we can see clearly how this prophecy was fulfilled. Jesus was:

Forsaken by Judas, who betrayed Him (Luke Ch.22 vs. 3 - 6).

Forsaken by His disciples. In Gethsemane 'all the disciples forsook him, and fled'.[2]

Forsaken by Peter, who denied that he even knew Jesus (Luke Ch.22 vs. 54 - 62).

Forsaken by the chief priests, the spiritual rulers of the people. In Luke Ch.23 it is recorded that when given the opportunity to have either Jesus or a murderer released, they chose Barabbas. Jesus had been accused of blasphemy. He was beaten, spat upon, flogged, crowned with thorns and then crucified. The agony of all this was compounded by the pain of being forsaken by His friends and by those who hated Him.

Forsaken by His Father

However, Jesus would descend into an even deeper valley of anguish when, on the cross, He suffered the traumatic experience of being forsaken by His Father. It caused Him to cry out, 'My God, my God, why hast thou forsaken me?'[3] It was bad enough to have been forsaken by His friends and enemies, but to be forsaken by His own Father must have broken His heart. In His distress He asked, "Father, for what reason have you deserted me?"

By becoming our sin-bearer and substitute Jesus became liable to the punishment and penalty our sins deserved. This penalty included the shedding of His blood and separation from His Father. He was forsaken by His Father because He 'bare our sins in his own body on the tree'.[4] On the cross 'He was wounded for our transgressions, he was bruised for our iniquities: the chastisement of our peace was upon him'.[5] His Father was laying on Him 'the iniquity of us all'.[6]

Fellowship with His Father would not be restored until Jesus had paid in full the penalty for our sins. His Father would not have abandoned Him to His tormentors or severed the bond of fellowship with His Son if it had not been necessary. However, it was necessary, in order that Jesus might fully undergo the punishment due to our sins.

No Other Way

If there had been any other way by which sin could be dealt with, then Christ would not have had to endure such suffering. If salvation could be merited through our involvement in religious activities or good works then the sacrifice of the Lamb of God was not necessary. If forgiveness of sins could be earned by any other means then there was no need for Jesus to shed His blood. However, the Scriptures make it clear that 'without shedding of blood is no remission'.[7] This means that without the shedding of Christ's blood there would be no release from sin and its guilt. It also means that there would be no remission of the punishment for sins. So it was necessary for Jesus to lay down His life in sacrifice, as there is no other way by which sinners can be saved. Jesus Himself said, 'I am the way, the truth, and the life: no man cometh unto the Father, but by me'.[8]

All of Your Sins

The Scriptures leave us in no doubt concerning the fact that when Christ died on the cross as our substitute He paid the penalty for not just some, or even most of our sins, but for all of them. John emphasises this when he says, 'The blood of Jesus Christ his Son cleanseth us from ALL sin.[9] Being now justified by his blood, we shall be saved from wrath through him'.[10] We are 'accepted in the beloved [Jesus], in whom we have redemption through his blood, the forgiveness of sins'.[11] He has 'washed us from our sins in his own blood'.[12]

Something to Consider

Because Jesus paid the penalty for your sins by the shedding of His blood, you can now be forgiven. Why not ask Him to forgive you and trust Him to save you today?

Lesson 12

The Resurrection of Jesus Christ

Luke Chapter 24

'He is Not Here, but is Risen'

These words declare the central doctrine of Christian Theology, namely the fact that Jesus Christ died, was buried and later rose from the dead. In Luke Ch.24 vs. 6 and 7 we are reminded of Jesus' own prediction concerning His death and resurrection. (Please read Luke Ch. 9 v. 22 and Ch. 18 vs. 31 – 34). In Ch. 24 vs. 25 – 27 Jesus explains that His death and resurrection are a central message of the Old Testament. The apostle Paul emphasises the fact that Jesus was 'declared to be the Son of God with power, according to the spirit of holiness, by the resurrection from the dead'.[1]

When Paul wrote to the Church in Corinth he reminded them of a Creed of the early Church which included the resurrection as an integral part of the gospel. Several eyewitnesses had testified to the fact that they had seen the risen Saviour, and Paul highlighted this by reminding the Corinthians that 'Christ died for our sins according to the scriptures; and that he was buried, and that he rose again the third day according to the scriptures: And that he was seen of Cephas, then of the twelve: After that he was seen of above five hundred brethren at once...After that he was seen of James; then of all the apostles. And last of all he was seen of me'.[2] Paul emphasised the importance of the resurrection of Jesus by insisting that 'if Christ be not raised, your faith is vain; ye are yet in your sins. Then they also which are fallen asleep in Christ are perished'.[3]

Christ's Resurrection and Our Resurrection

Paul goes so far as to say that without the resurrection there is no hope for the future. He concludes that if Jesus was not raised from the dead then His followers have no hope of resurrection. The apostle then goes on to highlight the fact that Christ did, in fact, rise from the dead and that this guarantees our resurrection. He enthusiastically declares, 'Now is Christ risen from the dead, and become the firstfruits of them that slept. For since by man came death, by man came also the resurrection of the dead. For as in Adam all die, even so in Christ shall all be made alive'.[4] He highlights the fact that 'He which raised up the Lord Jesus shall raise up us also by Jesus'.[5]

The Scriptures make it clear that the resurrection of Christ guarantees the resurrection of everyone. Those who have died trusting Christ as Saviour will be resurrected unto eternal life, while those who have died in their sins will be resurrected unto eternal torment in hell. Jesus said they 'shall come forth; they that have done good, unto the resurrection of life; and they that have done evil, unto the resurrection of damnation'.[6]

The Resurrection and Salvation

Paul also shows the importance of the resurrection in the salvation of sinners. He reminds us that 'if thou shalt confess with thy mouth the Lord Jesus, and shalt believe in thine heart that God hath raised him from the dead, thou shalt be saved'.[7] In fact, he identifies the resurrection of Christ as the basis of the gospel message.

Paul preached the need for repentance and highlighted the fact that sinners will one day be judged by the resurrected Christ. He leaves us in no doubt concerning the fact that God 'now commandeth all men everywhere to repent: Because he hath appointed a day, in the which he will judge the world in righteousness by that man whom he hath ordained; whereof he hath given assurance unto all men, in that he hath raised him from the dead'.[8]

The Resurrection and the Assurance of Salvation

The resurrection of Jesus Christ from the dead is the foundation upon which the assurance of salvation is built. The resurrection is God's seal of guarantee to everyone who has put their faith in Christ.

They know their sins are forgiven. They know that if God the Father had not been satisfied with the Atonement rendered by His Son for our sins, He would not have raised Him from the dead. As Peter preached on the day of Pentecost many of the Jews were convicted by the guilt of their sin. 'What shall we do?'[9] they asked. Peter assured them that their sins would be forgiven if they repented. He knew that Christ's resurrection was proof that the sins of all who would repent and put their faith in the Saviour had been dealt with at Calvary.

They know that they have a Saviour who lives for evermore to intercede for them. 'He [Christ] is able also to save them to the uttermost that come unto God by him, seeing he ever liveth to make intercession for them'.[10]

They know they have a Saviour who has said, 'I will never leave thee, nor forsake thee'.[11]

They know that Christ's resurrection guarantees that their bodies, too, will one day rise from the grave. Concerning those who are still alive on earth at the end, Paul says, 'We shall not all sleep, but we shall all be changed, In a moment, in the twinkling of an eye, at the last trump: for the trumpet shall sound, and the dead shall be raised incorruptible, and we shall be changed.[12] For the Lord himself shall descend from heaven with a shout, with the voice of the archangel, and with the trump of God: and the dead in Christ shall rise first: Then we which are alive and remain shall be caught up together with them in the clouds, to meet the Lord in the air: and so shall we ever be with the Lord'.[13]

Something to Consider

What must you do in order to be saved?
(a) **Repent** of your sins. This means sincere sorrow for your sins. It also means you have decided to change your ways.
(b) **Believe** that Christ paid the penalty for your sins when He died on the cross as your substitute. 'Believe on [put you faith in] the Lord Jesus Christ, and thou shalt be saved'.[14]
(c) **Ask** the Lord to forgive you and to save you, and trust Him to do so. 'For whosoever shall call upon the name of the Lord shall be saved'.[15]

'What manner of Man is this!'

The Scriptures make it clear that the baby born to the Virgin Mary in a stable in Bethlehem is none other than the eternally begotten Son of God, who is one in nature with the Father and the Holy Spirit. He is 'the image of the invisible God, the firstborn of every creature: For by him were all things created, that are in heaven, and that are in earth, visible and invisible, whether they be thrones, or dominions, or principalities, or powers: all things were created by him, and for him: And he is before all things, and by him all things consist'.[1] He is 'the brightness of his [God's] glory, and the express image of his person'.[2] God the Son assumed or took upon Himself human nature.

The Ministry of Jesus

He was tempted by the devil (Ch. 4 vs. 1 – 14).
He cast out demons (Ch. 4 vs. 33 – 37).
He healed people of leprosy and various illnesses (Ch. 5 vs. 12 – 15).
He healed a man who came through the roof (Ch. 5 vs. 17 – 26).
He has power to forgive sins (Ch. 5 vs. 20 – 24).
He interrupted a funeral and raised a widow's son to life (Ch. 7 vs. 11 – 16).
The wind and the waves obeyed Him (Ch. 8 vs. 22 – 25).
He raised a twelve year old girl from the dead (Ch. 8 vs. 41, 42, 49 – 56).
A woman who touched His garment was healed (Ch. 8 vs. 43 – 48).
He fed five thousand people with five loaves and two fish (Ch. 9 vs. 12 – 17).
He blessed little children (Ch. 18 vs. 15 – 17).
He wept over the unbelief in Jerusalem (Ch. 19 vs. 29 – 44).
He hunted the money changers out of the temple (Ch. 19 vs. 45, 46).
In Gethsemane His sweat was like drops of blood (Ch. 22 v. 44).
He was betrayed by a kiss from one of His own disciples (Ch. 22 vs. 47, 48).
Another one of His disciples denied he even knew Jesus (Ch. 22 vs. 54 – 62).
He was falsely accused and condemned (Ch. 22 v. 54 – Ch. 23 v. 24).
He was held captive while a murderer was released (Ch. 23 v. 25).

The Crucifixion, Resurrection and Ascension of Jesus

Jesus was crucified along with two criminals (Ch. 23 vs. 32, 33).
Jesus promised to save one of the criminals (Ch. 23 vs. 39 – 43).
Jesus died upon the cross (Ch 23 vs. 44 – 46).
He was taken down from the cross and laid in a tomb (Ch. 23 vs. 50 – 54).
Three days after His crucifixion Jesus rose from the dead (Ch. 24 vs. 1 – 12).
He appeared to His disciples on a number of occasions (Ch. 24 vs. 13 – 49).

The apostle Paul tells us that 'Christ died for our sins, according to the scriptures; And that he was buried, and that he rose again the third day according to the scriptures: And that he was seen of Cephas, then of the twelve; After that, he was seen of above five hundred brethren at once; of whom the greater part remain unto this present, but some are fallen asleep. After that, he was seen of James; then of all the apostles. And last of all he was seen of me also'.[3]

Jesus ascended to heaven (Luke Ch.24 vs. 50 – 53), but He will come back again (Luke Ch. 17 vs. 22 – 37). In the Book of Acts Luke reminds us of the last conversation Jesus had with His disciples before He ascended to heaven. He told His disciples that God would equip and enable them to proclaim the gospel. He said, 'Ye shall receive power after that the Holy Ghost is come upon you: and ye shall be witnesses unto me both in Jerusalem, and in all Judaea, and in Samaria, and unto the uttermost part of the earth'.[4]   The disciples were also reminded of the fact that Christ would one day return. 'While they beheld, he was taken up; and a cloud received him out of their sight. And while they looked steadfastly toward heaven as he went up, behold, two men stood by them in white apparel; Which also said, Ye men of Galilee, why stand ye gazing up into heaven? This same Jesus, which is taken up from you into heaven, shall so come in like manner as ye have seen him go into heaven'.[5]

The Purpose of Christ's Incarnation

God the Son came into the world for a specific purpose. 'Christ Jesus came into the world to save sinners'.[6] The Scriptures make it clear that 'when we were yet without strength, in due time Christ died for the ungodly'.[7] We are left in no doubt concerning the fact that 'while we were yet sinners, Christ died for us.[8] Being now justified by his blood, we shall be saved from wrath through him.[9] By whom we have now received the atonement'.[10] Jesus died for the ungodly. He died for sinners. He died for His enemies. He died for us.

In his Gospel, the apostle John says, 'There are also many other things which Jesus did, the which, if they should be written every one, I suppose that even the world itself could not contain the books that should be written'.[11]

The Pardon Purchased by Christ

Jesus laid down His life for us so that we could be reconciled to God. He made atonement for our sins. We can now be justified. We can now be declared to be 'not guilty'. We can be saved from wrath, saved from sin's penalty and saved from everlasting suffering in hell. Jesus took upon Himself the guilt of the sins of all who will repent and put their faith in Him (trust Him, rely upon Him and depend upon Him for salvation). He became their substitute and died in their place to pay the penalty for their sins. Through His death Jesus purchased for them a pardon. This pardon is now offered to repentant sinners as a free gift. It cannot be earned, bought or merited. 'The wages of sin is death; but the gift of God is eternal life through Jesus Christ our Lord'.[12]

Something to Consider

Eternal life is a free gift from God. The Lord is now offering this free gift to you. Will you accept this free gift today? 'Come now, and let us reason together, saith the Lord: though your sins be as scarlet, they shall be as white as snow; though they be red like crimson, they shall be as wool'.[13]

'Where is your Faith?'

Dear Friend,

I trust you have been thinking about this question and seriously considering your answer. As you have been reading through Luke's Gospel and the Bible lessons you have been left in no doubt concerning the fact that God loves you and desires to save your soul. The Scriptures tell us that 'all have sinned, and come short of the glory of God'.[1] This includes you! Maybe you think your sins are not serious and will cause you no problems. But there is a problem, for 'your iniquities have separated between you and your God, and your sins have hid His face from you, that he will not hear'.[2] The good news is that God the Father sent His only begotten Son, the Lord Jesus Christ, into the world to rescue you. 'Christ Jesus came into the world to save sinners'.[3] Jesus said, 'I am come to seek and to save that which was lost'.[4] Jesus suffered and died upon the cross as a substitute for all who will repent of their sins and put their faith in Him.

A Penalty Paid and a Pardon Offered

Through His death on the cross Jesus paid the penalty for the guilt of our sins. He secured for us a pardon. Friend, this pardon can be put to your account if you:

(a) *Acknowledge the fact that you are a sinner.* 'There is not a just man upon earth, that doeth good, and sinneth not'.[5]

(b) *Confess your sins to God.* 'If we confess our sins, he is faithful and just to forgive us our sins, and to cleanse us from all unrighteousness'.[6]

(c) *Repent of your sins.* This includes not only sorrow for sins but also a determination to turn away from sin and to return to God. 'Repent...and be converted, that your sins may be blotted out'.[7]

(d) *Acknowledge the fact that salvation is found in Christ alone.* 'Neither is there salvation in any other: For there is none other name under heaven given among men, whereby we must be saved'.[8] Jesus said, 'I am the way, the truth, and the life: no man cometh unto the Father, but by me'.[9]

(e) *Put you faith in Jesus (depend upon Him for your salvation).*
Believe that He died as your substitute, paying in full the penalty for the guilt of your sins. 'He was wounded for our transgressions, he was bruised for our iniquities; the chastisement of our peace was upon him; and with his stripes we are healed'.[10]

According to the Scriptures Christ was 'delivered for our offences, and was raised again for our justification.[11] Therefore being justified by faith, we have peace with God through our Lord Jesus Christ'.[12] Jesus said, 'Behold, I stand at the door, and knock: if any man hear my voice, and open the door, I will come in to him, and will sup with him, and he with me'.[13] Why not put your faith in Christ and ask Him to come into your life as Saviour and Lord? When this happens you become a Christian.

He is Able

Maybe you are wondering if you would be able to live the Christian life. But the Scriptures make it clear that Jesus 'is able also to save them to the uttermost that come unto God by him, seeing he ever liveth to make intercession for them'.[14] The Lord is not only able to save, but He is 'able to keep you from falling, and to present you faultless before the presence of his glory with exceeding joy'.[15] God can save you and keep you. He is 'able to make all grace abound toward you'.[16] The risen Saviour, the Lord Jesus Christ, is in heaven as our representative and continues to work on our behalf in the following ways:

He is our high priest. 'We have such an high priest, who is set on the right hand of the throne of the Majesty in the heavens'.[17]

He is our mediator. 'For there is one God, and one mediator between God and men, the man Christ Jesus'.[18]

He makes intercession for us. 'He ever liveth to make intercession for them'.[19]

He is our advocate (our legal representative, one who speaks in our defence). 'If any man sin, we have an advocate with the Father, Jesus Christ the righteous'.[20]

Not on our Own

The Lord does not expect us to live the Christian life in our own strength. He said, 'I will never leave thee, nor forsake thee'.[21] The Holy Spirit indwells all believers and empowers them to live the Christian life. God supplies, on a daily basis, the grace needed to deal with the trials and temptations they may face. The assurance of salvation removes the fear of death, the grave and hell. Fear is replaced by joy and rejoicing.

Something to Consider

Where is your faith?
Friend, why not put your faith in Christ and begin a new life today? 'If any man be in Christ, he is a new creature: old things are passed away; behold, all things are become new'.[22]

The Hour is Coming

The hour is coming in which you will have to leave your family, friends and neighbours behind.

The hour is coming in which you will have to leave all of your plans, aspirations and dreams behind.

The hour is coming in which you will have to leave all of your wealth, property and possessions behind. You may be prosperous and popular, but 'what shall it profit a man, if he shall gain the whole world, and lose his own soul?'[1]

The hour is coming in which many will understand what the Lord meant when He said, 'I have called, and ye refused; I have stretched out my hand, and no man regarded.[2] When I called, ye did not answer.[3] And ye will not come to me, that ye might have life'.[4]

The hour is coming in which you will no longer have the opportunity to respond to God's offer of salvation. 'The Lord said, My spirit shall not always strive with man'.[5]

The hour is coming in which you will die. 'What man is he that liveth, and shall not see death?'[6]

The hour is coming in which you will have to stand before the Judgement Seat of God. 'It is appointed unto men once to die, but after this the judgement'.[7]

The hour is coming in which 'all that are in the graves shall hear his voice, And shall come forth; they that have done good, unto the resurrection of life; and they that have done evil, unto the resurrection of damnation'.[8]

The hour is coming in which the resurrected multitude will hear God, the righteous Judge, passing sentence. To those who died in the faith, (who were trusting Christ as Saviour) He will say, 'Come, ye blessed of my Father, inherit the kingdom prepared for you from the foundation of the world'.[9] To those who died in their sins, (who refused or rejected God's offer of salvation) He will say, 'Depart from me, ye cursed, into everlasting fire, prepared for the devil and his angels'.[10] What will God say to YOU on Judgement Day?

Something to Consider

The hour is coming in which your opportunity to receive Christ as your Saviour will have passed and it will then be too late.

How can You be Saved?

According to the Scriptures we are all sinners and need the Saviour. This includes people of every religious persuasion and people who do not even believe in the existence of God, for 'there is none righteous, no, not one.'[1] For all have sinned, and come short of the glory of God.[2] The wages of sin is death'.[3]

'Who then can be saved?'[4] YOU can!

HOW can you be saved? You can be saved if you repent of your sins and put your faith in Jesus. Repentance includes sorrow for your sins, a determination to abandon your old sinful lifestyle and a resolve to follow the Lord. Faith in Christ as Saviour includes the belief that the guilt of your sins was put to His account, and also that the pardon Jesus purchased when He bore the penalty for those sins will be put to your account when you depend upon Him alone for your salvation.

Something to Consider

The Scriptures leave us in no doubt concerning the fact that you cannot be saved by good works, church membership, sacraments or religious activities. Eternal life cannot be earned or merited. Salvation is found in Christ alone. Jesus said, 'I am the way, the truth, and the life: no man cometh unto the Father, but by me'.[5]

Knocking and Calling

Jesus said, 'Behold, I stand at the door, and knock: if any man hear my voice, and open the door, I will come in to him, and will sup with him, and he with me'.[1] The Saviour is standing outside of your life. However, He is knocking and wants to come in. He is not only knocking, but He is also calling. Jesus said, 'If any man hear my voice…' He is calling you by name, and asking you to invite Him into your life as Saviour and Lord.

Something to Consider

Today is your day of opportunity, so 'today if ye will hear his voice, harden not your hearts.[2] Behold, NOW is the accepted time; behold, NOW is the day of salvation'.[3]

Why not ask Christ to save you today?

The Gospel of Luke

Chapter One

Introduction

1 Forasmuch as many have taken in hand to set forth in order a declaration of those things which are most surely believed among us,

2 Even as they delivered them unto us, which from the beginning were eyewitnesses, and ministers of the word;

3 It seemed good to me also, having had perfect understanding of all things from the very first, to write unto thee in order, most excellent Theophilus,

4 That thou mightest know the certainty of those things, wherein thou hast been instructed.

The Birth of John the Baptist Foretold

5 THERE was in the days of Herod, the king of Judaea, a certain priest named Zacharias, of the course of Abia: and his wife was of the daughters of Aaron, and her name was Elisabeth.

6 And they were both righteous before God, walking in all the commandments and ordinances of the Lord blameless.

7 And they had no child, because that Elisabeth was barren, and they both were now well stricken in years.

8 And it came to pass, that while he executed the priest's office before God in the order of his course,

9 According to the custom of the priest's office, his lot was to burn incense when he went into the temple of the Lord.

10 And the whole multitude of the people were praying without at the time of incense.

11 And there appeared unto him an angel of the Lord standing on the right side of the altar of incense.

12 And when Zacharias saw him, he was troubled, and fear fell upon him.

13 But the angel said unto him, Fear not, Zacharias: for thy prayer is heard; and thy wife Elisabeth shall bear thee a son, and thou shalt call his name John.

14 And thou shalt have joy and gladness; and many shall rejoice at his birth.

15 For he shall be great in the sight of the Lord, and shall drink neither wine nor strong drink; and he shall be filled with the Holy Ghost, even from his mother's womb.

16 And many of the children of Israel shall he turn to the Lord their God.

17 And he shall go before him in the spirit and power of Elias, to turn the hearts of the fathers to the children, and the disobedient to the wisdom of the just; to make ready a people prepared for the Lord.

18 And Zacharias said unto the angel, Whereby shall I know this? for I am an old man, and my wife well stricken in years.

19 And the angel answering said unto him, I am Gabriel, that stand in the presence of God; and am sent to speak unto thee, and to shew thee these glad tidings.

20 And, behold, thou shalt be dumb, and not able to speak, until the day that these things shall be performed, because thou believest not my words, which shall be fulfilled in their season.

21 And the people waited for Zacharias, and marvelled that he tarried so long in the temple.

22 And when he came out, he could not speak unto them: and they perceived that he had seen a vision in the temple: for he beckoned unto them, and remained speechless.

23 And it came to pass, that, as soon as the days of his ministration were accomplished, he departed to his own house.

24 And after those days his wife Elisabeth conceived, and hid herself five months, saying,

25 Thus hath the Lord dealt with me in the days wherein he looked on me, to take away my reproach among men.

The Angel Gabriel Visits the Virgin Mary

26 And in the sixth month the angel Gabriel was sent from God unto a city of Galilee, named Nazareth,

27 To a virgin espoused to a man whose name was Joseph, of the house of David; and the virgin's name was Mary.

28 And the angel came in unto her, and said, Hail, thou that art highly favoured, the Lord is with thee: blessed art thou among women.

29 And when she saw him, she was troubled at his saying, and cast in her
   mind what manner of salutation this should be.
30 And the angel said unto her, Fear not, Mary: for thou hast found favour
   with God.
31 And, behold, thou shalt conceive in thy womb, and bring forth a son,
   and shalt call his name JESUS.
32 He shall be great, and shall be called the Son of the Highest: and the
   Lord God shall give unto him the throne of his father David:
33 And he shall reign over the house of Jacob for ever; and of his kingdom
   there shall be no end.
34 Then said Mary unto the angel, How shall this be, seeing I know not a
   man?
35 And the angel answered and said unto her, The Holy Ghost shall come
   upon thee, and the power of the Highest shall overshadow thee:
   therefore also that holy thing which shall be born of thee shall be
   called the Son of God.
36 And, behold, thy cousin Elisabeth, she hath also conceived a son in her
   old age: and this is the sixth month with her, who was called barren.
37 For with God nothing shall be impossible.
38 And Mary said, Behold the handmaid of the Lord; be it unto me
   according to thy word. And the angel departed from her.

Mary Visits her Cousin

39 And Mary arose in those days, and went into the hill country with haste,
   into a city of Juda;
40 And entered into the house of Zacharias, and saluted Elisabeth.
41 And it came to pass, that, when Elisabeth heard the salutation of Mary,
   the babe leaped in her womb; and Elisabeth was filled with the Holy
   Ghost:
42 And she spake out with a loud voice, and said, Blessed art thou among
   women, and blessed is the fruit of thy womb.
43 And whence is this to me, that the mother of my Lord should come to
   me?
44 For, lo, as soon as the voice of thy salutation sounded in mine ears, the
   babe leaped in my womb for joy.

45 And blessed is she that believed: for there shall be a performance of those things which were told her from the Lord.

46 And Mary said, My soul doth magnify the Lord,

47 And my spirit hath rejoiced in God my Saviour.

48 For he hath regarded the low estate of his handmaiden: for, behold, from henceforth all generations shall call me blessed.

49 For he that is mighty hath done to me great things; and holy is his name.

50 And his mercy is on them that fear him from generation to generation.

51 He hath shewed strength with his arm; he hath scattered the proud in the imagination of their hearts.

52 He hath put down the mighty from their seats, and exalted them of low degree.

53 He hath filled the hungry with good things; and the rich he hath sent empty away.

54 He hath holpen his servant Israel, in remembrance of his mercy;

55 As he spake to our fathers, to Abraham, and to his seed for ever.

56 And Mary abode with her about three months, and returned to her own house.

The Birth of John the Baptist

57 Now Elisabeth's full time came that she should be delivered; and she brought forth a son.

58 And her neighbours and her cousins heard how the Lord had shewed great mercy upon her; and they rejoiced with her.

59 And it came to pass, that on the eight day they came to circumcise the child; and they called him Zacharias, after the name of his father.

60 And his mother answered and said, Not so; but he shall be called John.

61 And they said unto her, There is none of thy kindred that is called by this name.

62 And they made signs to his father, how he would have him called.

63 And he asked for a writing table, and wrote, saying, His name is John. And they marvelled all.

64 And his mouth was opened immediately, and his tongue loosed, and he spake, and praised God.

65 And fear came on all that dwelt round about them: and all these sayings were noised abroad throughout all the hill country of Judaea.

66 And all they that heard them laid them up in their hearts, saying, What manner of child shall this be! And the hand of the Lord was with him.

Zacharias Prophesies

67 And his father Zacharias was filled with the Holy Ghost, and prophesied, saying,

68 Blessed be the Lord God of Israel; for he hath visited and redeemed his people,

69 And hath raised up an horn of salvation for us in the house of his servant David;

70 As he spake by the mouth of his holy prophets, which have been since the world began:

71 That we should be saved from our enemies, and from the hand of all that hate us;

72 To perform the mercy promised to our fathers, and to remember his holy covenant;

73 The oath which he sware to our father Abraham,

74 That he would grant unto us, that we being delivered out of the hand of our enemies might serve him without fear,

75 In holiness and righteousness before him, all the days of our life.

76 And thou, child, shalt be called the prophet of the Highest: for thou shalt go before the face of the Lord to prepare his ways;

77 To give knowledge of salvation unto his people by the remission of their sins,

78 Through the tender mercy of our God; whereby the dayspring from on high hath visited us,

79 To give light to them that sit in darkness and in the shadow of death, to guide our feet into the way of peace.

80 And the child grew, and waxed strong in spirit, and was in the deserts till the day of his shewing unto Israel.

Chapter Two

The Birth of Jesus

1 And it came to pass in those days, that there went out a decree from Cesar Augustus, that all the world should be taxed.

2 (And this taxing was first made when Cyrenius was governor of Syria.)

3 And all went to be taxed, every one into his own city.

4 And Joseph also went up from Galilee, out of the city of Nazareth, into Judaea, unto the city of David, which is called Bethlehem; (because he was of the house and lineage of David:)

5 To be taxed with Mary his espoused wife, being great with child.

6 And so it was, that, while they were there, the days were accomplished that she should be delivered.

7 And she brought forth her first-born son, and wrapped him in swaddling clothes, and laid him in a manger; because there was no room for them in the inn.

Angels Appear to the Shepherds

8 And there were in the same country shepherds abiding in the field, keeping watch over their flock by night.

9 And, lo, the angel of the Lord came upon them, and the glory of the Lord shone round about them: and they were sore afraid.

10 And the angel said unto them, Fear not: for, behold, I bring you good tidings of great joy, which shall be to all people.

11 For unto you is born this day in the city of David a Saviour, which is Christ the Lord.

12 And this shall be a sign unto you; Ye shall find the babe wrapped in swaddling clothes, lying in a manger.

13 And suddenly there was with the angel a multitude of the heavenly host praising God, and saying,

14 Glory to God in the highest, and on earth peace, good will toward men.

15 And it came to pass, as the angels were gone away from them into heaven, the shepherds said one to another, Let us now go even unto Bethlehem, and see this thing which is come to pass, which the Lord hath made known unto us.

16 And they came with haste, and found Mary, and Joseph, and the babe lying in a manger.

17 And when they had seen it, they made known abroad the saying which was told them concerning this child.

18 And all they that heard it wondered at those things which were told them by the shepherds.

19 But Mary kept all these things, and pondered them in her heart.

20 And the shepherds returned, glorifying and praising God for all the things that they had heard and seen, as it was told unto them.

Jesus Presented in the Temple

21 And when eight days were accomplished for the circumcising of the child, his name was called JESUS, which was so named of the angel before he was conceived in the womb.

22 And when the days of her purification according to the law of Moses were accomplished, they brought him to Jerusalem, to present him to the Lord;

23 (As it is written in the law of the Lord, Every male that openeth the womb shall be called holy to the Lord;)

24 And to offer a sacrifice according to that which is said in the law of the Lord, A pair of turtledoves, or two young pigeons.

Simeon and Anna

25 And, behold, there was a man in Jerusalem, whose name was Simeon; and the same man was just and devout, waiting for the consolation of Israel: and the Holy Ghost was upon him.

26 And it was revealed unto him by the Holy Ghost, that he should not see death, before he had seen the Lord's Christ.

27 And he came by the Spirit into the temple: and when the parents brought in the child Jesus, to do for him after the custom of the law,

28 Then took he him up in his arms, and blessed God, and said,

29 Lord, now lettest thou thy servant depart in peace, according to thy word:

30 For mine eyes have seen thy salvation,

31 Which thou hast prepared before the face of all people;

32 A light to lighten the Gentiles, and the glory of thy people Israel.

33 And Joseph and his mother marvelled at those things which were spoken of him.

34 And Simeon blessed them, and said unto Mary his mother, Behold, this child is set for the fall and rising again of many in Israel; and for a sign which shall be spoken against;

35 (Yea, a sword shall pierce through thy own soul also,) that the thoughts of many hearts may be revealed.

36 And there was one Anna, a prophetess, the daughter of Phanuel, of the tribe of Aser: she was of a great age, and had lived with an husband seven years from her virginity;

37 And she was a widow of about fourscore and four years, which departed not from the temple, but served God with fastings and prayers night and day.

38 And she coming in that instant gave thanks likewise unto the Lord, and spake of him to all them that looked for redemption in Jerusalem.

39 And when they had performed all things according to the law of the Lord, they returned into Galilee, to their own city Nazareth.

40 And the child grew, and waxed strong in spirit, filled with wisdom: and the grace of God was upon him.

'I must be about My Father's Business'

41 Now his parents went to Jerusalem every year at the feast of the passover.

42 And when he was twelve years old, they went up to Jerusalem after the custom of the feast.

43 And when they had fulfilled the days, as they returned, the child Jesus tarried behind in Jerusalem; and Joseph and his mother knew not of it.

44 But they, supposing him to have been in the company, went a day's journey; and they sought him among their kinsfolk and acquaintance.

45 And when they found him not, they turned back again to Jerusalem, seeking him.

46 And it came to pass, that after three days they found him in the temple, sitting in the midst of the doctors, both hearing them, and asking them questions.

47 And all that heard him were astonished at his understanding and
answers.

48 And when they saw him, they were amazed: and his mother said unto
him, Son, why hast thou thus dealt with us? behold, thy father and I
have sought thee sorrowing.

49 And he said unto them, How is it that ye sought me? wist ye not that I
must be about my Father's business?

50 And they understood not the saying which he spake unto them.

51 And he went down with them, and came to Nazareth, and was subject
unto them: but his mother kept all these sayings in her heart.

52 And Jesus increased in wisdom and stature, and in favour with God and
man.

Chapter Three

The Voice of one Crying in the Wilderness

1 Now in the fifteenth year of the reign of Tiberius Caesar, Pontius Pilate
being governor of Judaea, and Herod being tetrarch of Galilee, and
his brother Philip tetrarch of Ituraea and of the region of Trachonitis,
and Lysanias the tetrarch of Abilene,

2 Annas and Caiaphas being the high priests, the word of God came unto
John the son of Zacharias in the wilderness.

3 And he came into all the country about Jordan, preaching the baptism of
repentance for the remission of sins;

4 As it is written in the book of the words of Esaias the prophet, saying,
The voice of one crying in the wilderness, Prepare ye the way of the
Lord, make his paths straight.

5 Every valley shall be filled, and every mountain and hill shall be brought
low; and the crooked shall be made straight, and the rough ways shall
be made smooth;

6 And all flesh shall see the salvation of God.

7 Then said he to the multitude that came forth to be baptized of him, O
generation of vipers, who hath warned you to flee from the wrath to
come?

8 Bring forth therefore fruits worthy of repentance, and begin not to say within yourselves, We have Abraham to our father: for I say unto you, That God is able of these stones to raise up children unto Abraham.

9 And now also the axe is laid unto the root of the trees: every tree therefore which bringeth not forth good fruit in hewn down, and cast into the fire.

10 And the people asked him, saying, What shall we do then?

11 He answereth and saith unto them, He that hath two coats, let him impart to him that hath none; and he that hath meat, let him do likewise.

12 Then came also publicans to be baptized, and said unto him, Master, what shall we do?

13 And he said unto them, Exact no more than that which is appointed you.

14 And the soldiers likewise demanded of him, saying, And what shall we do? And he said unto them, Do violence to no man, neither accuse any falsely; and be content with your wages.

15 And as the people were in expectation, and all men mused in their hearts of John, whether he were the Christ, or not;

16 John answered, saying unto them all, I indeed baptize you with water; but one mightier than I cometh, the latchet of whose shoes I am not worthy to unloose: he shall baptize you with the Holy Ghost and with fire:

17 Whose fan is in his hand, and he will thoroughly purge his floor, and will gather the wheat into his garner; but the chaff he will burn with fire unquenchable.

18 And many other things in his exhortation preached he unto the people.

19 But Herod the tetrarch, being reproved by him for Herodias his brother Philip's wife, and for all the evils which Herod had done,

20 Added yet this above all, that he shut up John in prison.

Jesus is Baptized by John

21 Now when all the people were baptized, it came to pass, that Jesus also being baptized, and praying, the heaven was opened,

22 And the Holy Ghost descended in a bodily shape like a dove upon him, and a voice came from heaven, which said, Thou art my beloved Son; in thee I am well pleased.

The Genealogy of Jesus

23 And Jesus himself began to be about thirty years of age, being (as was supposed) the son of Joseph, which was the son of Heli,

24 Which was the son of Matthat, which was the son of Levi, which was the son of Melchi, which was the son of Janna, which was the son of Joseph,

25 Which was the son of Mattathias, which was the son of Amos, which was the son of Naum, which was the son of Esli, which was the son of Nagge,

26 Which was the son of Maath, which was the son of Mattathias, which was the son of Semei, which was the son of Joseph, which was the son of Juda,

27 Which was the son of Joanna, which was the son of Rhesa, which was the son of Zorobabel, which was the son of Salathiel, which was the son of Neri,

28 Which was the son of Melchi, which was the son of Addi, which was he son of Cosam, which was the son of Elmodam, which was the son of Er,

29 Which was the son of Jose, which was the son of Eliezer, which was the son of Jorim, Which was the son of Matthat, which was the son of Levi,

30 Which was the son of Simeon, which was the son of Juda, which was the son of Joseph, which was the son of Jonan, which was the son of Eliakim,

31 Which was the son of Melea, which was the son of Menan, which was the son of Mattatha, which was the son of Nathan, which was the son of David,

32 Which was the son of Jesse, which was the son of Obed, which was the son of Booz, which was the son of Salmon, which was the son of Naasson,

33 Which was the son of Aminadab, which was the son of Aram, which was the son of Esrom, which was the son of Phares, which was the son of Juda,

34 Which was the son of Jacob, which was the son of Isaac, which was the son of Abraham, which was the son of Thara, which was the son of Nachor,

35 Which was the son of Saruch, which was the son of Ragau, which was the son of Phalec, which was the son of Heber, which was the son of Sala,

36 Which was the son of Cainan, which was the son of Arphaxad, which was the son of Sem, which was the son of Noe, which was the son of Lamech,

37 Which was the son of Mathusala, which was the son of Enoch, which was the son of Jared, which was the son of Maleleel, which was the son of Cainan,

38 Which was the son of Enos, which was the son of Seth, which was the son of Adam, which was the son of God.

Chapter Four

Jesus is Tempted by Satan

1 And Jesus being full of the Holy Ghost returned from Jordan, and was led by the Spirit into the wilderness,

2 Being forty days tempted of the devil. And in those days he did eat nothing: and when they were ended, he afterward hungered.

3 And the devil said unto him, If thou be the Son of God, command this stone that it be made bread.

4 And Jesus answered him, saying, It is written, That man shall not live by bread alone, but by every word of God.

5 And the devil, taking him up into an high mountain, shewed unto him all the kingdoms of the world in a moment of time.

6 And the devil said unto him, All this power will I give thee, and the glory of them: for that is delivered unto me; and to whomsoever I will I give it.

7 If thou therefore wilt worship me, all shall be thine.

8 And Jesus answered and said unto him, Get thee behind me, Satan: for it is written, Thou shalt worship the Lord thy God, and him only shalt thou serve.

9 And he brought him to Jerusalem, and set him on a pinnacle of the temple, and said unto him, If thou be the Son of God, cast thyself down from hence:

10 For it is written, He shall give his angels charge over thee, to keep thee:

11 And in their hands they shall bear thee up, lest at any time thou dash thy foot against a stone.

12 And Jesus answering said unto him, It is said, Thou shalt not tempt the Lord thy God.

13 And when the devil had ended all the temptation, he departed from him for a season.

'The Spirit of the Lord is upon Me'

14 And Jesus returned in the power of the Spirit into Galilee: and there went out a fame of him through all the region round about.

15 And he taught in their synagogues, being glorified of all.

16 And he came to Nazareth, where he had been brought up: and, as his custom was, he went into the synagogue on the sabbath day, and stood up for to read.

17 And there was delivered unto him the book of the prophet Esaias. And when he had opened the book, he found the place where it was written,

18 The Spirit of the Lord is upon me, because he hath anointed me to preach the gospel to the poor; he hath sent me to heal the broken-hearted, to preach deliverance to the captives, and recovering of sight to the blind, to set at liberty them that are bruised.

19 To preach the acceptable year of the Lord.

20 And he closed the book, and he gave it again to the minister, and sat down. And the eyes of all them that were in the synagogue were fastened on him.

21 And he began to say unto them, This day is this scripture fulfilled in your ears.

22 And all bare him witness, and wondered at the gracious words which proceeded out of his mouth. And they said, Is not this Joseph's son?

23 And he said unto them, Ye will surely say unto me this proverb, Physician, heal thyself: whatsoever we have heard done in Capernaum, do also here in thy country.

24 And he said, Verily I say unto you, No prophet is accepted in his own country.

25 But I tell you of a truth, many widows were in Israel in the days of Elias, when the heaven was shut up three years and six months, when great famine was throughout all the land;

26 But unto none of them was Elias sent, save unto Sarepta, a city of Sidon, unto a woman that was a widow.

27 And many lepers were in Israel in the time of Eliseus the prophet; and none of them was cleansed, saving Naaman the Syrian.

28 And all they in the synagogue, when they heard these things, were filled with wrath,

29 And rose up, and thrust him out of the city, and led him unto the brow of the hill whereon their city was built, that they might cast him down headlong.

30 But he passing through the midst of them went his way,

Jesus Casts out an Unclean Spirit

31 And came down to Capernaum, a city of Galilee, and taught them on the sabbath days.

32 And they were astonished at his doctrine: for his word was with power.

33 And in the synagogue there was a man, which had a spirit of an unclean devil, and cried out with a loud voice,

34 Saying, Let us alone; what have we to do with thee, thou Jesus of Nazareth? Art thou come to destroy us? I know thee who thou art; the Holy One of God.

35 And Jesus rebuked him, saying, Hold thy peace, and come out of him. And when the devil had thrown him in the midst, he came out of him, and hurt him not.

36 And they were all amazed, and spake among themselves, saying, What a word is this! For with authority and power he commandeth the unclean spirits and they come out.

37 And the fame of him went out into every place of the country round about.

Jesus Heals Many

38 And he arose out of the synagogue, and entered into Simon's house. And Simon's wife's mother was taken with a great fever; and they besought him for her.

39 And he stood over her, and rebuked the fever; and it left her: and immediately she arose and ministered unto them.

40 Now when the sun was setting, all they that had any sick with divers diseases brought them unto him; and he laid his hands on every one of them, and healed them.

41 And devils also came out of many, crying out, and saying, Thou art Christ the Son of God. And he rebuking them suffered them not to speak: for they knew that he was Christ.

42 And when it was day, he departed and went into a desert place: and the people sought him, and came unto him, and stayed him, that he should not depart from them.

43 And he said unto them, I must preach the kingdom of God to other cities also: for therefore am I sent.

44 And he preached in the synagogues of Galilee.

Chapter Five

Jesus Calls Fishermen to Follow Him

1 And it came to pass, that, as the people pressed upon him to hear the word of God, he stood by the lake of Gennesaret,

2 And saw two ships standing by the lake: but the fishermen were gone out of them, and were washing their nets.

3 And he entered into one of the ships, which was Simon's, and prayed him that he would thrust out a little from the land. And he sat down, and taught the people out of the ship.

4 Now when he had left speaking, he said unto Simon, Launch out into the deep, and let down your nets for a draught.

5 And Simon answering said unto him, Master, we have toiled all the night, and have taken nothing: nevertheless at thy word I will let down the net.

6 And when they had this done, they inclosed a great multitude of fishes: and their net brake.

7 And they beckoned unto their partners, which were in the other ship, that they should come and help them. And they came, and filled both the ships, so that they began to sink.

8 When Simon Peter saw it, he fell down at Jesus's knees, saying, Depart from me; for I am a sinful man, O Lord.

9 For he was astonished, and all that were with him, at the draught of fishes which they had taken:

10 And so was also James, and John, the sons of Zebedee, which were partners with Simon. And Jesus said unto Simon, Fear not; from henceforth thou shalt catch men.

11 And when they had brought their ships to land, they forsook all, and followed him.

A man with Leprosy is Cleansed by Jesus

12 And it came to pass, when he was in a certain city, behold a man full of leprosy: who seeing Jesus fell on his face, and besought him, saying, Lord, if thou wilt, thou canst make me clean.

13 And he put forth his hand, and touched him, saying, I will: be thou clean. And immediately the leprosy departed from him.

14 And he charged him to tell no man: but go, and shew thyself to the priest, and offer for thy cleansing, according as Moses commanded, for a testimony unto them.

15 But so much the more went there a fame abroad of him: and great multitudes came together to hear, and to be healed by him of their infirmities.

16 And he withdrew himself into the wilderness, and prayed.

Forgiveness and Healing of a Paralytic

17 And it came to pass on a certain day, as he was teaching, that there were Pharisees and doctors of the law sitting by, which were come out of every town of Galilee, and Judaea, and Jerusalem: and the power of the Lord was present to heal them.

18 And, behold, men brought in a bed a man which was taken with a palsy: and they sought means to bring him in, and to lay him before him.

19 And when they could not find by what way they might bring him in because of the multitude, they went upon the housetop, and let him down through the tiling with his couch into the midst before Jesus.

20 And when he saw their faith, he said unto him, Man, thy sins are forgiven thee.

21 And the scribes and the Pharisees began to reason, saying, Who is this which speaketh blasphemies? Who can forgive sins, but God alone?

22 But when Jesus perceived their thoughts, he answering said unto them, What reason ye in your hearts?

23 Whether is easier, to say, Thy sins be forgiven thee; or to say, Rise up and walk?

24 But that ye may know that the Son of man hath power upon earth to forgive sins, (he said unto the sick of the palsy,) I say unto thee, Arise, and take up thy couch, and go into thine house.

25 And immediately he rose up before them, and took up that whereon he lay, and departed to his own house, glorifying God.

26 And they were all amazed, and they glorified God, and were filled with fear, saying, We have seen strange things today.

Jesus Calls a Tax Collector to be His Disciple

27 And after these things he went forth, and saw a publican, named Levi, sitting at the receipt of custom: and he said unto him, Follow me.

28 And he left all, rose up, and followed him.

29 And Levi made him a great feast in his own house: and there was a great company of publicans and of others that sat down with them.

30 But their scribes and Pharisees murmured against his disciples, saying, Why do ye eat and drink with publicans and sinners?

31 And Jesus answering said unto them, They that are whole need not a physician; but they that are sick.

32 I came not to call the righteous, but sinners to repentance.

Christ Questioned about Fasting

33 And they said unto him, Why do the disciples of John fast often, and make prayers, and likewise the disciples of the Pharisees; but thine eat and drink?

34 And he said unto them, Can ye make the children of the bride-chamber fast, while the bridegroom is with them?

35 But the days will come, when the bridegroom shall be taken away from them, and then shall they fast in those days.

36 And he spake also a parable unto them; No man putteth a piece of a new garment upon an old; if otherwise, then both the new maketh a rent, and the piece that was taken out of the new agreeth not with the old.

37 And no man putteth new wine into old bottles; else the new wine will burst the bottles, and be spilled, and the bottles shall perish.

38 But new wine must be put into new bottles; and both are preserved.

39 No man also having drunk old wine straightway desireth new: for he saith, The old is better.

Chapter Six

Jesus is Lord of the Sabbath

1 And it came to pass on the second sabbath after the first, that he went through the corn fields; and his disciples plucked the ears of corn, and did eat, rubbing them in their hands.

2 And certain of the Pharisees said unto them, Why do ye that which is not lawful to do on the sabbath days?

3 And Jesus answering them said, Have ye not read so much as this, what David did, when himself was an hungred, and they which were with him;

4 How he went into the house of God, and did take and eat the shewbread, and gave also to them that were with him; which it is not lawful to eat but for the priests alone?

5 And he said unto them, That the Son of man is Lord also of the sabbath.

6 And it came to pass also on another sabbath, that he entered into the synagogue and taught: and there was a man whose right hand was withered.

7 And the scribes and Pharisees watched him, whether he would heal on the sabbath day; that they might find an accusation against him.

8 But he knew their thoughts, and said to the man which had the withered hand, Rise up, and stand forth in the midst. And he arose and stood forth.

9 Then said Jesus unto them, I will ask you one thing; Is it lawful on the sabbath days to do good, or to do evil? to save life, or to destroy it?

10 And looking round about upon them all, he said unto the man, Stretch forth thy hand. And he did so: and his hand was restored whole as the other.

11 And they were filled with madness, and communed one with another what they might do to Jesus.

Jesus Chose Twelve

12 And it came to pass in those days, that he went out into a mountain to pray, and continued all night in prayer to God.

13 And when it was day, he called unto him his disciples: and of them he chose twelve, whom also he named apostles;

14 Simon, (whom he also named Peter,) and Andrew his brother, James and John, Philip and Bartholomew,

15 Matthew and Thomas, James the son of Alphaeus, and Simon called Zelotes,

16 And Judas the brother of James, and Judas Iscariot, which also was the traitor.

There went Virtue out of Him, and Healed them all

17 And he came down with them, and stood in the plain, and the company of his disciples, and a great multitude of people out of all Judaea and Jerusalem, and from the sea coast of Tyre and Sidon, which came to hear him, and to be healed of their diseases;

18 And they that were vexed with unclean spirits: and they were healed.

19 And the whole multitude sought to touch him: for there went virtue out of him, and healed them all.

The Beatitudes

20 And he lifted up his eyes on his disciples, and said, Blessed be ye poor: for yours is the kingdom of God.
21 Blessed are ye that hunger now: for ye shall be filled. Blessed are ye that weep now: for ye shall laugh.
22 Blessed are ye, when men shall hate you, and when they shall separate you from their company, and shall reproach you, and cast out your name as evil, for the Son of man's sake.
23 Rejoice ye in that day, and leap for joy: for, behold, your reward is great in heaven: for in the like manner did their fathers unto the prophets.

Woes Pronounced

24 But woe unto you that are rich! for ye have received your consolation.
25 Woe unto you that are full! for ye shall hunger. Woe unto you that laugh now! for ye shall mourn and weep.
26 Woe unto you, when all men shall speak well of you! for so did their fathers to the false prophets.

Love Your Enemies

27 But I say unto you which hear, Love your enemies, do good to them which hate you.
28 Bless them that curse you, and pray for them which despitefully use you.
29 And unto him that smiteth thee on the one cheek offer also the other; and him that taketh away thy cloak forbid not to take thy coat also.
30 Give to every man that asketh of thee; and of him that taketh away thy goods ask them not again.
31 And as ye would that men should do to you, do ye also to them likewise.
32 For if ye love them which love you, what thank have ye? for sinners also love those that love them.
33 And if ye do good to them which do good to you, what thank have ye? for sinners also do even the same.

34 And if ye lend to them of whom ye hope to receive, what thank have ye? for sinners also lend to sinners, to receive as much again.
35 But love your enemies, and do good, and lend, hoping for nothing again; and your reward shall be great, and ye shall be the children of the Highest: for he is kind unto the unthankful and to the evil.
36 Be ye therefore merciful, as your Father also is merciful.

Judging Others

37 Judge not, and ye shall not be judged: condemn not, and ye shall not be condemned: forgive, and ye shall be forgiven:
38 Give, and it shall be given unto you; good measure, pressed down, and shaken together, and running over, shall men give into your bosom. For with the same measure that ye mete withal it shall be measured to you again.
39 And he spake a parable unto them, Can the blind lead the blind? shall they not both fall into the ditch?
40 The disciple is not above his master: but every one that is perfect shall be as his master.
41 And why beholdest thou the mote that is in thy brother's eye, but perceivest not the beam that is in thine own eye?
42 Either how canst thou say to thy brother, Brother, let me pull out the mote that is in thine eye, when thou thyself beholdest not the beam that is in thine own eye? Thou hypocrite, cast out first the beam out of thine own eye, and then shalt thou see clearly to pull out the mote that is in thy bother's eye.

A Tree and its Fruit

43 For a good tree bringeth not forth corrupt fruit; neither doth a corrupt tree bring forth good fruit.
44 For every tree is known by his own fruit. For of thorns men do not gather figs, nor of a bramble bush gather they grapes.
45 A good man out of the good treasure of his heart bringeth forth that which is good; and an evil man out of the evil treasure of his heart bringeth forth that which is evil: for of the abundance of the heart the mouth speaketh.

Wise and Foolish Builders

46 And why call ye me, Lord, Lord, and do not the things which I say?

47 Whosoever cometh to me, and heareth my sayings, and doeth them, I will shew you to whom he is like:

48 He is like a man which built an house, and digged deep, and laid the foundation on a rock: and when the flood arose, the stream beat vehemently upon that house, and could not shake it: for it was founded upon a rock.

49 But he that heareth, and doeth not, is like a man that without a foundation built an house upon the earth; against which the stream did beat vehemently, and immediately it fell; and the ruin of that house was great.

Chapter Seven

The Centurion's Faith

1 Now when he had ended all his sayings in the audience of all the people, he entered into Capernaum.

2 And a certain centurion's servant, who was dear unto him, was sick, and ready to die.

3 And when he heard of Jesus, he sent unto him the elders of the Jews, beseeching him that he would come and heal his servant.

4 And when they came to Jesus, they besought him instantly, saying, That he was worthy for whom he should do this:

5 For he loveth our nation, and he hath built us a synagogue.

6 Then Jesus went with them. And when he was now not far from the house, the centurion sent friends to him, saying unto him, Lord, trouble not thyself: for I am not worthy that thou shouldest enter under my roof:

7 Wherefore neither thought I myself worthy to come unto thee: but say in a word, and my servant shall be healed.

8 For I also am a man set under authority, having under me soldiers, and I say unto one, Go, and he goeth; and to another, Come, and he cometh; and to my servant, Do this, and he doeth it.

9 When Jesus heard these things, he marvelled at him, and turned him about, and said unto the people that followed him, I say unto you, I have not found so great faith, no, not in Israel.

10 And they that were sent, returning to the house, found the servant whole that had been sick.

The Dead Man sat up and began to Speak

11 And it came to pass the day after, that he went into a city called Nain; and many of his disciples went with him, and much people.

12 Now when he came nigh to the gate of the city, behold, there was a dead man carried out, the only son of his mother, and she was a widow: and much people of the city was with her.

13 And when the Lord saw her, he had compassion on her, and said unto her, Weep not.

14 And he came and touched the bier: and they that bare him stood still. And he said, Young man, I say unto thee, Arise.

15 And he that was dead sat up, and began to speak. And he delivered him to his mother.

16 And there came a fear on all: and they glorified God, saying, That a great prophet is risen up among us; and, That God hath visited his people.

17 And this rumour of him went forth throughout all Judaea, and throughout all the region round about.

John the Baptist's Question

18 And the disciples of John shewed him of all these things.

19 And John calling unto him two of his disciples sent them to Jesus, saying, Art thou he that should come? or look we for another?

20 When the men were come unto him, they said, John Baptist hath sent us unto thee, saying, Art thou he that should come? or look we for another?

21 And in that same hour he cured many of their infirmities and plagues, and of evil spirits; and unto many that were blind he gave sight.

22 Then Jesus answering said unto them, Go your way, and tell John what things ye have seen and heard; how that the blind see, the lame walk, the lepers are cleansed, the deaf hear, the dead are raised, to the poor the gospel is preached.

23 And blessed is he, whosoever shall not be offended in me.

24 And when the messengers of John were departed, he began to speak unto the people concerning John, What went ye out into the wilderness for to see? A reed shaken in the wind?

25 But what went ye out for to see? A man clothed in soft raiment? Behold, they which are gorgeously apparelled, and live delicately, are in kings' courts.

26 But what went ye out for to see? A prophet? Yea, I say unto you, and much more than a prophet.

27 This is he, of whom it is written, Behold, I send my messenger before thy face, which shall prepare thy way before thee.

28 For I say unto you, Among those that are born of women there is not a greater prophet than John the Baptist: but he that is least in the kingdom of God is greater than he.

29 And all the people that heard him, and the publicans, justified God, being baptized with the baptism of John.

30 But the Pharisees and lawyers rejected the counsel of God against themselves, being not baptized of him.

31 And the Lord said, Whereunto then shall I liken the men of this generation? And to what are they like?

32 They are like unto children sitting in the marketplace, and calling one to another, and saying, We have piped unto you, and ye have not danced; we have mourned to you, and ye have not wept.

33 For John the Baptist came neither eating bread nor drinking wine; and ye say, He hath a devil.

34 The Son of man is come eating and drinking; and ye say, Behold a gluttonous man, and a wine-bibber, a friend of publicans and sinners!

35 But wisdom is justified of all her children.

Jesus Forgives a Sinful Woman

36 And one of the Pharisees desired him that he would eat with him. And he went into the Pharisee's house, and sat down to meat.

37 And behold, a woman in the city, which was a sinner, when she knew that Jesus sat at meat in the Pharisee's house, brought an alabaster box of ointment,

38 And stood at his feet behind him weeping, and began to wash his feet with tears, and did wipe them with the hairs of her head, and kissed his feet, and anointed them with the ointment.

39 Now when the Pharisee which had bidden him saw it, he spake within himself, saying, This man, if he were a prophet, would have known who and what manner of woman this is that touched him: for she is a sinner.

40 And Jesus answering said unto him, Simon, I have somewhat to say unto thee. And he saith, Master, say on.

41 There was a certain creditor which had two debtors: the one owed five hundred pence, and the other fifty.

42 And when they had nothing to pay, he frankly forgave them both. Tell me therefore, which of them will love him most?

43 Simon answered and said, I suppose he, to whom he forgave most. And he said unto him, Thou hast rightly judged.

44 And he turned to the woman, and said unto Simon, Seest thou this woman? I entered into thine house, thou gavest me no water for my feet: but she hath washed my feet with tears, and wiped them with the hairs of her head.

45 Thou gavest me no kiss: but this woman since the time I came in hath not ceased to kiss my feet.

46 My head with oil thou didst not anoint: but this woman hath anointed my feet with ointment.

47 Wherefore I say unto thee, Her sins, which are many, are forgiven; for she loved much: but to whom little is forgiven, the same loveth little.

48 And he said unto her, Thy sins are forgiven.

49 And they that sat at meat with him began to say within themselves, Who is this that forgiveth sins also?

50 And he said to the woman, Thy faith hath saved thee; go in peace.

Chapter Eight

The Sower

1 And it came to pass afterward, that he went throughout every city and village, preaching and shewing the glad tidings of the kingdom of God: and the twelve were with him,

2 And certain women, which had been healed of evil spirits and infirmities, Mary called Magdalene, out of whom went seven devils,

3 And Joanna, the wife of Chuza Herod's steward, and Susanna, and many others, which ministered unto him out of their substance.

4 And when much people were gathered together, and were come to him out of every city, he spake by a parable:

5 A sower went out to sow his seed: and as he sowed, some fell by the way side; and it was trodden down, and the fowls of the air devoured it.

6 And some fell upon a rock; and as soon as it was sprung up, it withered away, because it lacked moisture.

7 And some fell among thorns; and the thorns sprang up with it, and choked it.

8 And other fell on good ground, and sprang up, and bare fruit an hundredfold. And when he had said these things, he cried, He that hath ears to hear, let him hear.

9 And his disciples asked him, saying, What might this parable be?

10 And he said, Unto you it is given to know the mysteries of the kingdom of God: but to others in parables; that seeing they might not see, and hearing they might not understand.

11 Now the parable is this: The seed is the word of God.

12 Those by the way side are they that hear; then cometh the devil, and taketh away the word out of their hearts, lest they should believe and be saved.

13 They on the rock are they, which, when they hear, receive the word with joy; and these have no root, which for a while believe, and in time of temptation fall away.

14 And that which fell among thorns are they, which, when they have heard, go forth, and are choked with cares and riches and pleasures of this life, and bring no fruit to perfection.

15 But that on the good ground are they, which in an honest and good heart, having heard the word, keep it, and bring forth fruit with patience.

The Lighted Candle

16 No man, when he hath lighted a candle, covereth it with a vessel, or putteth it under a bed; but setteth it on a candlestick, that they which enter in may see the light.

17 For nothing is secret, that shall not be made manifest; neither any thing hid, that shall not be known and come abroad.

18 Take heed therefore how ye hear: for whosoever hath, to him shall be given; and whosoever hath not, from him shall be taken even that which he seemeth to have.

Jesus' Mother and Brothers

19 Then came to him his mother and his brethren, and could not come at him for the press.

20 And it was told him by certain which said, Thy mother and thy brethren stand without, desiring to see thee.

21 And he answered and said unto them, My mother and my brethren are these which hear the word of God, and do it.

Jesus Calms a Storm

22 Now it came to pass on a certain day, that he went into a ship with his disciples: and he said unto them, Let us go over unto the other side of the lake. And they launched forth.

23 But as they sailed he fell asleep: and there came down a storm of wind on the lake; and they were filled with water, and were in jeopardy.

24 And they came to him, and awoke him, saying, Master, master, we perish. Then he arose, and rebuked the wind and the raging of the water: and they ceased, and there was a calm.

25 And he said unto them, Where is your faith? And they being afraid wondered, saying one to another, What manner of man is this! For he commandeth even the winds and the water, and they obey him.

A Demon-Possessed Man is Healed

26 And they arrived at the country of the Gadarenes, which is over against Galilee.

27 And when he went forth to land, there met him out of the city a certain man, which had devils long time, and ware no clothes, neither abode in any house, but in the tombs.

28 And when he saw Jesus, he cried out, and fell down before him, and with a loud voice said, What have I to do with thee, Jesus, thou Son of God most high? I beseech thee, torment me not.

29 (For he had commanded the unclean spirit to come out of the man. For oftentimes it had caught him: and he was kept bound with chains and in fetters; and he brake the bands, and was driven of the devil into the wilderness.)

30 And Jesus asked him, saying, What is thy name? And he said, Legion: because many devils were entered into him.

31 And they besought him that he would not command them to go out into the deep.

32 And there was there an herd of many swine feeding on the mountain: and they besought him that he would suffer them to enter into them. And he suffered them.

33 Then went the devils out of the man, and entered into the swine: and the herd ran violently down a steep place into the lake, and were choked.

34 When they that fed them saw what was done, they fled, and went and told it in the city and in the country.

35 Then they went out to see what was done; and came to Jesus, and found the man, out of whom the devils were departed, sitting at the feet of Jesus, clothed, and in his right mind: and they were afraid.

36 They also which saw it told them by what means he that was possessed of the devils was healed.

37 Then the whole multitude of the country of the Gadarenes round about besought him to depart from them; for they were taken with great fear: and he went up into the ship, and returned back again.

38 Now the man out of whom the devils were departed besought him that he might be with him: but Jesus sent him away, saying,

39 Return to thine own house, and shew how great things God hath done unto thee. And he went his way, and published throughout the whole city how great things Jesus had done unto him.

A Dead Girl and a Suffering Woman

40 And it came to pass, that when Jesus was returned, the people gladly received him: for they were all waiting for him.
41 And, behold, there came a man named Jairus, and he was a ruler of the synagogue: and he fell down at Jesus' feet, and besought him that he would come into his house:
42 For he had only one daughter, about twelve years of age, and she lay a dying. But as he went the people thronged him.
43 And a woman having an issue of blood twelve years, which had spent all her living upon physicians, neither could be healed of any,
44 Came behind him, and touched the border of his garment: and immediately her issue of blood stanched.
45 And Jesus said, Who touched me? When all denied, Peter and they that were with him said, Master, the multitude throng thee and press thee, and sayest thou, Who touched me?
46 And Jesus said, Somebody hath touched me: for I perceive that virtue is gone out of me.
47 And when the woman saw that she was not hid, she came trembling, and falling down before him, she declared unto him before all the people for what cause she had touched him, and how she was healed immediately.
48 And he said unto her, Daughter, be of good comfort: thy faith hath made thee whole; go in peace.
49 While he yet spake, there cometh one from the ruler of the synagogue's house, saying to him, Thy daughter is dead; trouble not the Master.
50 But when Jesus heard it, he answered him, saying, Fear not: believe only, and she shall be made whole.
51 And when he came into the house, he suffered no man to go in, save Peter, and James, and John, and the father and the mother of the maiden.

52 And all wept, and bewailed her: but he said, Weep not; she is not dead, but sleepeth.

53 And they laughed him to scorn, knowing that she was dead.

54 And he put them all out, and took her by the hand, and called, saying, Maid, arise.

55 And her spirit came again, and she arose straightway: and he commanded to give her meat.

56 And her parents were astonished: but he charged them that they should tell no man what was done.

Chapter Nine

The Twelve Apostles Sent out

1 Then he called his twelve disciples together, and gave them power and authority over all devils, and to cure diseases.

2 And he sent them to preach the kingdom of God, and to heal the sick.

3 And he said unto them, Take nothing for your journey, neither staves, nor scrip, neither bread, neither money; neither have two coats apiece.

4 And whatsoever house ye enter into, there abide, and thence depart.

5 And whosoever will not receive you, when ye go out of that city, shake off the very dust from your feet for a testimony against them.

6 And they departed, and went through the towns, preaching the gospel, and healing every where.

John the Baptist Beheaded

7 Now Herod the tetrarch heard of all that was done by him: and he was perplexed, because that it was said of some, that John was risen from the dead;

8 And of some, that Elias had appeared; and of others, that one of the old prophets was risen again.

9 And Herod said, John have I beheaded: but who is this, of whom I hear such things? And he desired to see him.

Jesus Feeds Five Thousand

10 And the apostles, when they were returned, told him all that they had
done. And he took them, and went aside privately into a desert place
belonging to the city called Bethsaida.

11 And the people, when they knew it, followed him: and he received
them, and spake unto them of the kingdom of God, and healed them
that had need of healing.

12 And when the day began to wear away, then came the twelve, and said
unto him, Send the multitude away, that they may go into the towns
and country round about, and lodge, and get victuals: for we are here
in a desert place.

13 But he said unto them, Give ye them to eat. And they said, We have no
more but five loaves and two fishes; except we should go and buy
meat for all this people.

14 For they were about five thousand men. And he said to his disciples,
Make them sit down by fifties in a company.

15 And they did so, and made them all sit down.

16 Then he took the five loaves and the two fishes, and looking up to
heaven, he blessed them, and brake, and gave to the disciples to set
before the multitude.

17 And they did eat, and were all filled: and there was taken up of
fragments that remained to them twelve baskets.

Peter's Confession of Christ

18 And it came to pass, as he was alone praying, his disciples were with
him: and he asked them, saying, Whom say the people that I am?

19 They answering said, John the Baptist; but some say, Elias; and others
say, that one of the old prophets is risen again.

20 He said unto them, But whom say ye that I am? Peter answering said,
The Christ of God.

21 And he straitly charged them, and commanded them to tell no man that thing;

22 Saying, The Son of man must suffer many things, and be rejected of the elders and chief priests and scribes, and be slain, and be raised the third day.

Conditions of Discipleship

23 And he said to them all, If any man will come after me, let him deny himself, and take up his cross daily, and follow me.

24 For whosoever will save his life shall lose it: but whosoever will lose his life for my sake, the same shall save it.

25 For what is a man advantaged, if he gain the whole world, and lose himself, or be cast away?

26 For whosoever shall be ashamed of me and of my words, of him shall the Son of man be ashamed, when he shall come in his own glory, and in his Father's, and of the holy angels.

27 But I tell you of a truth, there be some standing here, which shall not taste of death, till they see the kingdom of God.

Jesus is Transfigured

28 And it came to pass about an eight days after these sayings, he took Peter and John and James, and went up into a mountain to pray.

29 And as he prayed, the fashion of his countenance was altered, and his raiment was white and glistering.

30 And, behold, there talked with him two men, which were Moses and Elias:

31 Who appeared in glory, and spake of his decease which he should accomplish at Jerusalem.

32 But Peter and they that were with him were heavy with sleep: and when they were awake, they saw his glory, and the two men that stood with him.

33 And it came to pass, as they departed from him, Peter said unto Jesus, Master, it is good for us to be here: and let us make three tabernacles; one for thee, and one for Moses, and one for Elias: not knowing what he said.

34 While he thus spake, there came a cloud, and overshadowed them: and they feared as they entered into the cloud.

35 And there came a voice out of the cloud, saying, This is my beloved Son: hear him.

36 And when the voice was past, Jesus was found alone. And they kept it close, and told no man in those days any of those things which they had seen.

A Boy is Healed

37 And it came to pass, that on the next day, when they were come down from the hill, much people met him.

38 And behold, a man of the company cried out, saying, Master, I beseech thee, look upon my son: for he is mine only child.

39 And lo, a spirit taketh him, and he suddenly crieth out; and it teareth him that he foameth again, and bruising him hardly departeth from him.

40 And I besought thy disciples to cast him out: and they could not.

41 And Jesus answering said, O faithless and perverse generation, how long shall I be with you, and suffer you? Bring thy son hither.

42 And as he was yet a coming, the devil threw him down, and tare him. And Jesus rebuked the unclean spirit, and healed the child, and delivered him again to his father.

43 And they were all amazed at the mighty power of God. But while they wondered every one at all things which Jesus did, he said to his disciples,

44 Let these sayings sink down into your ears: for the Son of man shall be delivered into the hands of men.

45 But they understood not this saying, and it was hid from them, that they perceived it not: and they feared to ask him of that saying.

Who will be the Greatest?

46 Then there arose a reasoning among them, which of them should be the greatest.

47 And Jesus, perceiving the thought of their heart, took a child, and set him by him,

48 And said unto them, Whosoever shall receive this child in my name receiveth me: and whosoever shall receive me receiveth him that sent me: for he that is least among you all, the same shall be great.

49 And John answered and said, Master, we saw one casting out devils in thy name; and we forbad him, because he followeth not with us.

50 And Jesus said unto him, Forbid him not: for he that is not against us is for us.

Samaritans Reject Jesus

51 And it came to pass, when the time was come that he should be received up, he stedfastly set his face to go to Jerusalem,

52 And sent messengers before his face: and they went, and entered into a village of the Samaritans, to make ready for him.

53 And they did not receive him, because his face was as though he would go to Jerusalem.

54 And when his disciples James and John saw this, they said, Lord, wilt thou that we command fire to come down from heaven, and consume them, even as Elias did?

55 But he turned, and rebuked them, and said, Ye know not what manner of spirit ye are of.

56 For the Son of man is not come to destroy men's lives, but to save them. And they went to another village.

Half-Hearted Followers

57 And it came to pass, that, as they went in the way, a certain man said unto him, Lord, I will follow thee whithersoever thou goest.

58 And Jesus said unto him, Foxes have holes, and the birds of the air have nests; But the Son of man hath not where to lay his head.

59 And he said unto another, Follow me. But he said, Lord, suffer me first to go and bury my father.

60 Jesus said unto him, Let the dead bury their dead: but go thou and preach the kingdom of God.

61 And another also said, Lord, I will follow thee; but let me first go bid them farewell, which are at home at my house.

62 And Jesus said unto him, No man, having put his hand to the plough, and looking back, is fit for the kingdom of God.

Chapter Ten

More Disciples Sent out

1 After these things the Lord appointed other seventy also, and sent them two and two before his face into every city and place, whither he himself would come.

2 Therefore said he unto them, The harvest truly is great, but the labourers are few: pray ye therefore the Lord of the harvest, that he would send forth labourers into his harvest.

3 Go your ways: behold, I send you forth as lambs among wolves.

4 Carry neither purse, nor scrip, nor shoes: and salute no man by the way.

5 And into whatsoever house ye enter, first say, Peace be to this house.

6 And if the son of peace be there, your peace shall rest upon it: if not, it shall turn to you again.

7 And in the same house remain, eating and drinking such things as they give: for the labourer is worthy of his hire. Go not from house to house.

8 And into whatsoever city ye enter, and they receive you, eat such things as are set before you:

9 And heal the sick that are therein, and say unto them, The kingdom of God is come nigh unto you.

10 But into whatsoever city ye enter, and they receive you not, go your ways out into the streets of the same, and say,

11 Even the very dust of your city, which cleaveth on us, we do wipe off against you: notwithstanding be ye sure of this, that the kingdom of God is come nigh unto you.

12 But I say unto you, that it shall be more tolerable in that day for Sodom, than for that city.

Jesus Denounces Impenitent Cities

13 Woe unto thee, Chorazin! Woe unto thee, Bethsaida! for if the mighty works had been done in Tyre and Sidon, which have been done in you, they had a great while ago repented, sitting in sackcloth and ashes.

14 But it shall be more tolerable for Tyre and Sidon at the judgment, than for you.

15 And thou, Capernaum, which art exalted to heaven, shalt be thrust down to hell.

16 He that heareth you heareth me; and he that despiseth you despiseth me; and he that despiseth me despiseth him that sent me.

The Disciples' Joy

17 And the seventy returned again with joy, saying, Lord, even the devils are subject unto us through thy name.

18 And he said unto them, I beheld Satan as lightning fall from heaven.

19 Behold, I give unto you power to tread on serpents and scorpions, and over all the power of the enemy: and nothing shall by any means hurt you.

20 Notwithstanding in this rejoice not, that the spirits are subject unto you; but rather rejoice, because your names are written in heaven.

Jesus Rejoices

21 In that hour Jesus rejoiced in spirit, and said, I thank thee, O Father, Lord of heaven and earth, that thou hast hid these things from the wise and prudent, and hast revealed them unto babes: even so, Father; for so it seemed good in thy sight.

22 All things are delivered to me of my Father: and no man knoweth who the Son is, but the Father; and who the Father is, but the Son, and he to whom the Son will reveal him.

23 And he turned him unto his disciples, and said privately, Blessed are the eyes which see the things that ye see:

24 For I tell you, that many prophets and kings have desired to see those things which ye see, and have not seen them; and to hear those things which ye hear, and have not heard them.

The Good Samaritan

25 And, behold, a certain lawyer stood up, and tempted him, saying, Master, what shall I do to inherit eternal life?

26 He said unto him, What is written in the law? how readest thou?

27 And he answering said, Thou shalt love the Lord thy God with all thy heart, and with all thy soul, and with all thy strength, and with all thy mind; and thy neighbour as thyself.

28 And he said unto him, Thou hast answered right: this do, and thou shalt live.

29 But he, willing to justify himself, said unto Jesus, And who is my neighbour?

30 And Jesus answering said, A certain man went down from Jerusalem to Jericho, and fell among thieves, which stripped him of his raiment, and wounded him, and departed, leaving him half dead.

31 And by chance there came down a certain priest that way: and when he saw him, he passed by on the other side.

32 And likewise a Levite, when he was at the place, came and looked on him, and passed by on the other side.

33 But a certain Samaritan, as he journeyed, came where he was: and when he saw him, he had compassion on him,

34 And went to him, and bound up his wounds, pouring in oil and wine, and set him on his own beast, and brought him to an inn, and took care of him.

35 And on the morrow when he departed, he took out two pence, and gave them to the host, and said unto him, Take care of him; and whatsoever thou spendest more, when I come again, I will repay thee.

36 Which now of these three, thinkest thou, was neighbour unto him that fell among the thieves?

37 And he said, He that shewed mercy on him. Then said Jesus unto him, Go, and do thou likewise.

Mary and Martha

38 Now it came to pass, as they went, that he entered into a certain village: and a certain woman named Martha received him into her house.

39 And she had a sister called Mary, which also sat at Jesus' feet, and heard his word.

40 But Martha was cumbered much about serving, and came to him, and said, Lord, dost thou not care that my sister hath left me to serve alone? Bid her therefore that she help me.

41 And Jesus answered and said unto her, Martha, Martha, thou art careful and troubled about many things:

42 But one thing is needful: and Mary hath chosen that good part, which shall not be taken away from her.

Chapter Eleven

The Lord's Prayer

1 And it came to pass, that, as he was praying in a certain place, when he ceased, one of his disciples said unto him, Lord, teach us to pray, as John also taught his disciples.

2 And he said unto them, When ye pray, say, Our Father which art in heaven, Hallowed by thy name. Thy kingdom come. Thy will be done, as in heaven, so in earth.

3 Give us day by day our daily bread.

4 And forgive us our sins; for we also forgive every one that is indebted to us. And lead us not into temptation; but deliver us from evil.

Three Loaves

5 And he said unto them, Which of you shall have a friend, and shall go unto him at midnight, and say unto him, Friend, lend me three loaves;

6 For a friend of mine in his journey is come to me, and I have nothing to set before him?

7 And he from within shall answer and say, Trouble me not: the door is now shut, and my children are with me in bed; I cannot rise and give thee.

8 I say unto you, Though he will not rise and give him, because he is his friend, yet because of his importunity he will rise and give him as many as he needeth.

Three-Fold Promise

9 And I say unto you, Ask, and it shall be given you; seek, and ye shall find; knock, and it shall be opened unto you.

10 For every one that asketh receiveth; and he that seeketh findeth; and to him that knocketh it shall be opened.

11 If a son shall ask bread of any of you that is a father, will he give him a stone? or if he ask a fish, will he for a fish give him a serpent?

12 Or if he shall ask an egg, will he offer him a scorpion?

13 If ye then, being evil, know how to give good gifts unto your children: how much more shall your heavenly Father give the Holy Spirit to them that ask him?

Jesus and Beelzebub

14 And he was casting out a devil, and it was dumb. And it came to pass, when the devil was gone out, the dumb spake; and the people wondered.

15 But some of them said, He casteth out devils through Beelzebub the chief of the devils.

16 And others, tempting him, sought of him a sign from heaven.

17 But he, knowing their thoughts, said unto them, Every kingdom divided against itself is brought to desolation; and a house divided against a house falleth.

18 If Satan also be divided against himself, how shall his kingdom stand? because ye say that I cast out devils through Beelzebub.

19 And if I by Beelzebub cast out devils, by whom do your sons cast them out? therefore shall they be your judges.

20 But if I with the finger of God cast out devils, no doubt the kingdom of God is come upon you.

21 When a strong man armed keepeth his palace, his goods are in peace:

22 But when a stronger than he shall come upon him, and overcome him, he taketh from him all his armour wherein he trusted, and divideth his spoils.

23 He that is not with me is against me: and he that gathereth not with me scattereth.

24 When the unclean spirit is gone out of a man, he walketh through dry places, seeking rest; and finding none, he saith, I will return unto my house whence I came out.

25 And when he cometh, he findeth it swept and garnished.

26 Then goeth he, and taketh to him seven other spirits more wicked than himself; and they enter in, and dwell there: and the last state of that man is worse than the first.

Hearing and Keeping God's Word

27 And it came to pass, as he spake these things, a certain woman of the company lifted up her voice, and said unto him, Blessed is the womb that bare thee, and the paps which thou hast sucked.

28 But he said, Yea rather, blessed are they that hear the word of God, and keep it.

Seeking a Sign

29 And when the people were gathered thick together, he began to say, This is an evil generation: they seek a sign; and there shall no sign be given it, but the sign of Jonas the prophet.

30 For as Jonas was a sign unto the Ninevites, so shall also the Son of man be to this generation.

31 The queen of the south shall rise up in the judgment with the men of this generation, and condemn them: for she came from the utmost parts of the earth to hear the wisdom of Solomon; and, behold, a greater than Solomon is here.

32 The men of Nineveh shall rise up in the judgment with this generation, and shall condemn it: for they repented at the preaching of Jonas; and behold, a greater than Jonas is here.

The Light of the Body

33 No man, when he hath lighted a candle, putteth it in a secret place, neither under a bushel, but on a candlestick, that they which come in may see the light.

34 The light of the body is the eye: therefore when thine eye is single, thy whole body also is full of light; but when thine eye is evil, thy body also is full of darkness.

35 Take heed therefore that the light which is in thee be not darkness.

36 If thy whole body therefore be full of light, having no part dark, the whole shall be full of light, as when the bright shining of a candle doth give thee light.

Woes Pronounced upon Hypocrites

37 And as he spake, a certain Pharisee besought him to dine with him: and he went in, and sat down to meat.

38 And when the Pharisee saw it, he marvelled that he had not first washed before dinner.

39 And the Lord said unto him, Now do ye Pharisees make clean the outside of the cup and the platter; but your inward part is full of ravening and wickedness.

40 Ye fools, did not he that made that which is without make that which is within also?

41 But rather give alms of such things as ye have; and, behold, all things are clean unto you.

42 But woe unto you, Pharisees! For ye tithe mint and rue and all manner of herbs, and pass over judgment and the love of God: these ought ye to have done, and not to leave the other undone.

43 Woe unto you, Pharisees! For ye love the uppermost seats in the synagogues, and greetings in the markets.

44 Woe unto you, scribes and Pharisees, hypocrites! For ye are as graves which appear not, and the men that walk over them are not aware of them.

45 Then answered one of the lawyers, and said unto him, Master, thus saying thou reproachest us also.

46 And he said, Woe unto you also, ye lawyers! For ye lade men with burdens grievous to be borne, and ye yourselves touch not the burdens with one of your fingers.

47 Woe unto you! For ye build the sepulchres of the prophets, and your fathers killed them.

48 Truly ye bear witness that ye allow the deeds of your fathers: for they indeed killed them, and ye build their sepulchres.

49 Therefore also said the wisdom of God, I will send them prophets and apostles, and some of them they shall slay and persecute:

50 That the blood of all the prophets, which was shed from the foundation of the world, may be required of this generation;

51 From the blood of Abel unto the blood of Zacharias, which perished between the altar and the temple: verily I say unto you, It shall be required of this generation.

52 Woe unto you, lawyers! For ye have taken away the key of knowledge: ye entered not in yourselves, and them that were entering in ye hindered.

53 And as he said these things unto them, the scribes and the Pharisees began to urge him vehemently, and to provoke him to speak of many things:

54 Laying wait for him, and seeking to catch something out of his mouth, that they might accuse him.

Chapter Twelve

Warnings and Encouragements

1 In the mean time, when there were gathered together an innumerable multitude of people, insomuch that they trode one upon another, he began to say unto his disciples first of all, Beware ye of the leaven of the Pharisees, which is hypocrisy.

2 For there is nothing covered, that shall not be revealed; neither hid, that shall not be known.

3 Therefore whatsoever ye have spoken in darkness shall be heard in the light; and that which ye have spoken in the ear in closets shall be proclaimed upon the housetops.

4 And I say unto you my friends, Be not afraid of them that kill the body, and after that have no more that they can do.

5 But I will forewarn you whom ye shall fear: Fear him, which after he hath killed hath power to cast into hell; yea, I say unto you, Fear him.

6 Are not five sparrows sold for two farthings, and not one of them is forgotten before God?

7 But even the very hairs of your head are all numbered. Fear not therefore: ye are of more value than many sparrows.

8 Also I say unto you, Whosoever shall confess me before men, him shall the Son of man also confess before the angels of God:

9 But he that denieth me before men shall be denied before the angels of God.

10 And whosoever shall speak a word against the Son of man, it shall be forgiven him: but unto him that blasphemeth against the Holy Ghost it shall not be forgiven.

11 And when they bring you unto the synagogues, and unto magistrates, and powers, take ye no thought how or what thing ye shall answer, or what ye shall say:

12 For the Holy Ghost shall teach you in the same hour what ye ought to say.

The Rich Fool

13 And one of the company said unto him, Master, speak to my brother, that he divide the inheritance with me.

14 And he said unto him, Man, who made me a judge or a divider over you?

15 And he said unto them, Take heed, and beware of covetousness: for a man's life consisteth not in the abundance of the things which he possesseth.

16 And he spake a parable unto them, saying, The ground of a certain rich man brought forth plentifully:

17 And he thought within himself, saying, What shall I do, because I have no room where to bestow my fruits?

18 And he said, This will I do: I will pull down my barns, and build greater; and there will I bestow all my fruits and my goods.

19 And I will say to my soul, Soul, thou hast much goods laid up for many years; take thine ease, eat, drink, and be merry.

20 But God said unto him, Thou fool, this night thy soul shall be required
of thee: then whose shall those things be, which thou hast provided?

21 So is he that layeth up treasure for himself, and is not rich toward God.

No Need to Worry

22 And he said unto his disciples, Therefore I say unto you, take no
thought for your life, what ye shall eat; neither for the body, what ye
shall put on.

23 The life is more than meat, and the body is more than raiment.

24 Consider the ravens: for they neither sow nor reap; which neither have
storehouse nor barn; and God feedeth them: how much more are ye
better than the fowls?

25 And which of you with taking thought can add to his stature one cubit?

26 If ye then be not able to do that thing which is least, why take ye
thought for the rest?

27 Consider the lilies how they grow: they toil not, they spin not; and yet I
say unto you, that Solomon in all his glory was not arrayed like one
of these.

28 If God then so clothe the grass, which is today in the field, and
tomorrow is cast into the oven; how much more will he clothe you,
O ye of little faith?

29 And seek not ye what ye shall eat, or what ye shall drink, neither be ye
of doubtful mind.

30 For all these things do the nations of the world seek after: and your
Father knoweth that ye have need of these things.

31 But rather seek ye the kingdom of God; and all these things shall be
added unto you.

32 Fear not, little flock; for it is the Father's good pleasure to give you the
kingdom.

33 Sell that ye have, and give alms; provide yourselves bags which wax not
old, a treasure in the heavens that faileth not, where no thief
approacheth, neither moth corrupteth.

34 For where your treasure is, there will your heart be also.

Readiness for The Lord's Return

35 Let your loins be girded about, and your lights burning;

36 And ye yourselves like unto men that wait for their lord, when he will return from the wedding; that when he cometh and knocketh, they may open unto him immediately.

37 Blessed are those servants, whom the lord when he cometh shall find watching; verily I say unto you, that he shall gird himself, and make them to sit down to meat, and will come forth and serve them.

38 And if he shall come in the second watch, or come in the third watch, and find them so, blessed are those servants.

39 And this know, that if the goodman of the house had known what hour the thief would come, he would have watched, and not have suffered his house to be broken through.

40 Be ye therefore ready also: for the Son of man cometh at an hour when ye think not.

41 Then Peter said unto him, Lord, speakest thou this parable unto us, or even to all?

42 And the Lord said, Who then is that faithful and wise steward, whom his lord shall make ruler over his household, to give them their portion of meat in due season?

43 Blessed is that servant, whom his lord when he cometh shall find so doing.

44 Of a truth I say unto you, that he will make him ruler over all that he hath.

45 But and if that servant say in his heart, My lord delayeth his coming; and shall begin to beat the menservants and maidens, and to eat and drink and to be drunken;

46 The lord of that servant will come in a day when he looketh not for him, and at an hour when he is not aware, and will cut him in sunder, and will appoint him his portion with the unbelievers.

47 And that servant, which knew his lord's will, and prepared not himself, neither did according to his will, shall be beaten with many stripes.

48 But he that knew not, and did commit things worthy of stripes, shall be beaten with few stripes. For unto whomsoever much is given, of him shall be much required: and to whom men have committed much, of him they will ask the more.

Division

49 I am come to send fire on the earth; and what will I, if it be already kindled?

50 But I have a baptism to be baptized with; and how am I straitened till it be accomplished!

51 Suppose ye that I am come to give peace on earth? I tell you, Nay; but rather division:

52 For from henceforth there shall be five in one house divided, three against two, and two against three.

53 The father shall be divided against the son, and the son against the father; the mother against the daughter, and the daughter against the mother; the mother in law against her daughter in law, and the daughter in law against her mother in law.

Lack of Spiritual Discernment

54 And he said also to the people, When ye see a cloud rise out of the west, straightway ye say, There cometh a shower; and so it is.

55 And when ye see the south wind blow, ye say, There will be heat; and it cometh to pass.

56 Ye hypocrites, ye can discern the face of the sky and of the earth; but how is it that ye do not discern this time?

57 Yea, and why even of yourselves judge ye not what is right?

58 When thou goest with thine adversary to the magistrate, as thou art in the way, give diligence that thou mayest be delivered from him: lest he hale thee to the judge, and the judge deliver thee to the officer, and the officer cast thee into prison.

59 I tell thee, thou shalt not depart thence, till thou hast paid the very last mite.

Chapter Thirteen

Repent or Perish

1 There were present at that season some that told him of the Galilaeans, whose blood Pilate had mingled with their sacrifices.

2 And Jesus answering said unto them, Suppose ye that these Galilaeans were sinners above all the Galilaeans, because they suffered such things?

3 I tell you, Nay; but, except ye repent, ye shall all likewise perish.

4 Or those eighteen, upon whom the tower in Siloam fell, and slew them, think ye that they were sinners above all men that dwelt in Jerusalem?

5 I tell you, Nay: but, except ye repent, ye shall all likewise perish.

The Barren Fig Tree

6 He spake also this parable; A certain man had a fig tree planted in his vineyard; and he came and sought fruit thereon, and found none.

7 Then said he unto the dresser of his vineyard, Behold, these three years I come seeking fruit on this fig tree, and find none: cut it down; why cumbereth it the ground?

8 And he answering said unto him, Lord, let it alone this year also, till I shall dig about it, and dung it:

9 And if it bear fruit, well: and if not, then after that thou shalt cut it down.

The Healing of a Crippled Woman

10 And he was teaching in one of the synagogues on the sabbath.

11 And behold, there was a woman which had a spirit of infirmity eighteen years, and was bowed together, and could in no wise lift up herself.

12 And when Jesus saw her, he called her to him, and said unto her, Woman, thou art loosed from thine infirmity.

13 And he laid his hands on her: and immediately she was made straight, and glorified God.

14 And the ruler of the synagogue answered with indignation, because that Jesus had healed on the sabbath day, and said unto the people, There are six days in which men ought to work: in them therefore come and be healed, and not on the sabbath day.

15 The Lord then answered him, and said, Thou hypocrite, doth not each one of you on the sabbath loose his ox or his ass from the stall, and lead him away to watering?

16 And ought not this woman, being a daughter of Abraham, whom Satan hath bound, lo, these eighteen years, be loosed from this bond on the sabbath day?

17 And when he had said these things, all his adversaries were ashamed: and all the people rejoiced for all the glorious things that were done by him.

The Mustard Seed and the Leaven

18 Then said he, Unto what is the kingdom of God like? And whereunto shall I resemble it?

19 It is like a grain of mustard seed, which a man took, and cast into his garden; and it grew, and waxed a great tree; and the fowls of the air lodged in the branches of it.

20 And again he said, Whereunto shall I liken the kingdom of God?

21 It is like leaven, which a woman took and hid in three measures of meal, till the whole was leavened.

Are there Few that be Saved?

22 And he went through the cities and villages, teaching, and journeying toward Jerusalem.

23 Then said one unto him, Lord, are there few that be saved? And he said unto them,

24 Strive to enter in at the strait gate: for many, I say unto you, will seek to enter in, and shall not be able.

25 When once the master of the house is risen up, and hath shut the door, and ye begin to stand without, and to knock at the door, saying, Lord, Lord, open unto us; and he shall answer and say unto you, I know you not whence ye are:

26 Then shall ye begin to say, We have eaten and drunk in thy presence, and thou hast taught in our streets.

27 But he shall say, I tell you, I know you not whence ye are; depart from me, all ye workers of iniquity.

28 There shall be weeping and gnashing of teeth, when ye shall see Abraham, and Isaac, and Jacob, and all the prophets, in the kingdom of God, and you yourselves thrust out.

29 And they shall come from the east, and from the west, and from the north, and from the south, and shall sit down in the kingdom of God.

30 And, behold, there are last which shall be first, and there are first which shall be last.

31 The same day there came certain of the Pharisees, saying unto him, Get thee out, and depart hence: for Herod will kill thee.

32 And he said unto them, Go ye, and tell that fox, Behold, I cast out devils, and I do cures today and tomorrow, and the third day I shall be perfected.

33 Nevertheless I must walk today, and tomorrow, and the day following: for it cannot be that a prophet perish out of Jerusalem.

Jesus Laments over Jerusalem

34 O Jerusalem, Jerusalem, which killest the prophets, and stonest them that are sent unto thee; how often would I have gathered thy children together, as a hen doth gather her brood under her wings, and ye would not!

35 Behold, your house is left unto you desolate: and verily I say unto you, Ye shall not see me, until the time come when ye shall say, Blessed is he that cometh in the name of the Lord.

Chapter Fourteen

Jesus Heals a man on the Sabbath

1 And it came to pass, as he went into the house of one of the chief Pharisees to eat bread on the sabbath day, that they watched him.

2 And, behold, there was a certain man before him which had the dropsy.

3 And Jesus answering spake unto the lawyers and Pharisees, saying, Is it lawful to heal on the sabbath day?

4 And they held their peace. And he took him, and healed him, and let him go:

5 And answered them, saying, Which of you shall have an ass or an ox fallen into a pit, and will not straightway pull him out on the sabbath day?

6 And they could not answer him again to these things.

He that Humbles himself shall be Exalted

7 And he put forth a parable to those which were bidden, when he marked how they chose out the chief rooms; saying unto them,

8 When thou art bidden of any man to a wedding, sit not down in the highest room; lest a more honourable man than thou be bidden of him;

9 And he that bade thee and him come and say to thee, Give this man place; and thou begin with shame to take the lowest room.

10 But when thou art bidden, go and sit down in the lowest room; that when he that bade thee cometh, he may say unto thee, Friend, go up higher: then shalt thou have worship in the presence of them that sit at meat with thee.

11 For whosoever exalteth himself shall be abased; and he that humbleth himself shall be exalted.

12 Then said he also to him that bade him, When thou makest a dinner or a supper, call not thy friends, nor thy brethren, neither thy kinsmen, nor thy rich neighbours; lest they also bid thee again, and a recompense be made thee.

13 But when thou makest a feast, call the poor, the maimed, the lame, the blind:

14 And thou shalt be blessed; for they cannot recompense thee: for thou shalt be recompensed at the resurrection of the just.

The Great Supper

15 And when one of them that sat at meat with him heard these things, he said unto him, Blessed is he that shall eat bread in the kingdom of God.

16 Then said he unto him, A certain man made a great supper, and bade many:

17 And sent his servant at supper time to say to them that were bidden, Come; for all things are now ready.

18 And they all with one consent began to make excuse. The first said unto him, I have bought a piece of ground, and I must needs go and see it: I pray thee have me excused.

19 And another said, I have bought five yoke of oxen, and I go to prove them: I pray thee have me excused.

20 And another said, I have married a wife, and therefore I cannot come.

21 So that servant came, and shewed his lord these things. Then the master of the house being angry said to his servant, Go out quickly into the streets and lanes of the city, and bring in hither the poor, and the maimed, and the halt, and the blind.

22 And the servant said, Lord, it is done as thou hast commanded, and yet there is room.

23 And the lord said unto the servant, Go out into the highways and hedges, and compel them to come in, that my house may be filled.

24 For I say unto you, That none of those men which were bidden shall taste of my supper.

Counting the Cost

25 And there went great multitudes with him: and he turned, and said unto them,

26 If any man come to me, and hate not his father, and mother, and wife, and children, and brethren, and sisters, yea, and his own life also, he cannot be my disciple.

27 And whosoever doth not bear his cross, and come after me, cannot be my disciple.

28 For which of you, intending to build a tower, sitteth not down first, and counteth the cost, whether he have sufficient to finish it?

29 Lest haply, after he hath laid the foundation, and is not able to finish it, all that behold it begin to mock him,
30 Saying, This man began to build, and was not able to finish.
31 Or what king, going to make war against another king, sitteth not down first, and consulteth whether he be able with ten thousand to meet him that cometh against him with twenty thousand?
32 Or else, while the other is yet a great way off, he sendeth an ambassage, and desireth conditions of peace.
33 So likewise, whosoever he be of you that forsaketh not all that he hath, he cannot be my disciple.

Tasteless Salt

34 Salt is good: but if the salt have lost his savour, wherewith shall it be seasoned?
35 It is neither fit for the land, nor yet for the dunghill; but men cast it out. He that hath ears to hear, let him hear.

Chapter Fifteen

The Lost Sheep

1 Then drew near unto him all the publicans and sinners for to hear him.
2 And the Pharisees and scribes murmured, saying, This man receiveth sinners, and eateth with them.
3 And he spake this parable unto them, saying,
4 What man of you, having an hundred sheep, if he lose one of them, doth not leave the ninety and nine in the wilderness, and go after that which is lost, until he find it?
5 And when he hath found it, he layeth it on his shoulders, rejoicing.
6 And when he cometh home, he calleth together his friends and neighbours, saying unto them, Rejoice with me; for I have found my sheep which was lost.
7 I say unto you, that likewise joy shall be in heaven over one sinner that repenteth, more than over ninety and nine just persons, which need no repentance.

The Lost Coin

8 Either what woman having ten pieces of silver, if she lose one piece, doth not light a candle, and sweep the house, and seek diligently till she find it?

9 And when she hath found it, she calleth her friends and her neighbours together, saying, Rejoice with me; for I have found the piece which I had lost.

10 Likewise, I say unto you, there is joy in the presence of the angels of God over one sinner that repenteth.

The Lost Son

11 And he said, A certain man had two sons:

12 And the younger of them said to his father, Father, give me the portion of goods that falleth to me. And he divided unto them his living.

13 And not many days after the younger son gathered all together, and took his journey into a far country, and there wasted his substance with riotous living.

14 And when he had spent all, there arose a mighty famine in that land; and he began to be in want.

15 And he went and joined himself to a citizen of that country; and he sent him into his fields to feed swine.

16 And he would fain have filled his belly with the husks that the swine did eat: and no man gave unto him.

17 And when he came to himself, he said, How many hired servants of my father's have bread enough and to spare, and I perish with hunger!

18 I will arise and go to my father, and will say unto him, Father, I have sinned against heaven, and before thee,

19 And am no more worthy to be called thy son: make me as one of thy hired servants.

20 And he arose, and came to his father. But when he was yet a great way off, his father saw him, and had compassion, and ran, and fell on his neck, and kissed him.

21 And the son said unto him, Father, I have sinned against heaven, and in thy sight, and am no more worthy to be called thy son.

22 But the father said to his servants, Bring forth the best robe, and put it on him; and put a ring on his hand, and shoes on his feet:

23 And bring hither the fatted calf, and kill it; and let us eat, and be merry:

24 For this my son was dead, and is alive again; he was lost, and is found. And they began to be merry.

25 Now his elder brother was in the field: and as he came and drew nigh to the house, he heard music and dancing.

26 And he called one of the servants, and asked what these things meant.

27 And he said unto him, Thy brother is come; and thy father hath killed the fatted calf, because he hath received him safe and sound.

28 And he was angry, and would not go in: therefore came his father out, and intreated him.

29 And he answering said to his father, Lo, these many years do I serve thee, neither transgressed I at any time thy commandment: and yet thou never gavest me a kid, that I might make merry with my friends:

30 But as soon as this thy son was come, which hath devoured thy living with harlots, thou hast killed for him the fatted calf.

31 And he said unto him, Son, thou art ever with me, and all that I have is thine.

32 It was meet that we should make merry, and be glad: for this thy brother was dead, and is alive again: and was lost, and is found.

Chapter Sixteen

The Unjust Steward

1 And he said also unto his disciples, There was a certain rich man, which had a steward; and the same was accused unto him that he had wasted his goods.

2 And he called him, and said unto him, How is it that I hear this of thee? give an account of thy stewardship; for thou mayest be no longer steward.

3 Then the steward said within himself, What shall I do? for my lord taketh away from me the stewardship: I cannot dig: to beg I am ashamed.

4 I am resolved what to do, that, when I am put out of the stewardship, they may receive me into their houses.

5 So he called every one of his lord's debtors unto him, and said unto the first, How much owest thou unto my lord?

6 And he said, An hundred measures of oil. And he said unto him, Take thy bill, and sit down quickly, and write fifty.

7 Then said he to another, And how much owest thou? And he said, An hundred measures of wheat. And he said unto him, Take thy bill, and write fourscore.

8 And the lord commended the unjust steward, because he had done wisely; for the children of this world are in their generation wiser than the children of light.

9 And I say unto you, Make to yourselves friends of the mammon of unrighteousness; that, when ye fail, they may receive you into everlasting habitations.

10 He that is faithful in that which is least is faithful also in much: and he that is unjust in the least is unjust also in much.

11 If therefore ye have not been faithful in the unrighteous mammon, who will commit to your trust the true riches?

12 And if ye have not been faithful in that which is another man's, who shall give you that which is your own?

13 No servant can serve two masters: for either he will hate the one, and love the other; or else he will hold to the one, and despise the other. Ye cannot serve God and mammon.

The Law, the Prophets and the Kingdom of God

14 And the Pharisees also, who were covetous, heard all these things: and they derided him.

15 And he said unto them, Ye are they which justify yourselves before men; but God knoweth your hearts: for that which is highly esteemed among men is abomination in the sight of God.

16 The law and the prophets were until John: since that time the kingdom of God is preached, and every man presseth into it.

17 And it is easier for heaven and earth to pass, than one tittle of the law to fail.

18 Whosoever putteth away his wife, and marrieth another, commiteth adultery; and whosoever marrieth her that is put away from her husband committeth adultery.

The Rich Man and the Beggar

19 There was a certain rich man, which was clothed in purple and fine
linen, and fared sumptuously every day:

20 And there was a certain beggar named Lazarus, which was laid at his
gate, full of sores,

21 And desiring to be fed with the crumbs which fell from the rich man's
table: moreover the dogs came and licked his sores.

22 And it came to pass, that the beggar died, and was carried by the angels
into Abraham's bosom: the rich man also died, and was buried;

23 And in hell he lift up his eyes, being in torments, and seeth Abraham
afar off, and Lazarus in his bosom.

24 And he cried and said, Father Abraham, have mercy on me, and send
Lazarus, that he may dip the tip of his finger in water, and cool my
tongue; for I am tormented in this flame.

25 But Abraham said, Son, remember that thou in thy lifetime receivedst
thy good things, and likewise Lazarus evil things: but now he is
comforted, and thou art tormented.

26 And beside all this, between us and you there is a great gulf fixed: so
that they which would pass from hence to you cannot; neither can
they pass to us, that would come from thence.

27 Then said he, I pray thee therefore, father, that thou wouldest send him
to my father's house;

28 For I have five brethren; that he may testify unto them, lest they also
come into this place of torment.

29 Abraham saith unto him, They have Moses and the prophets; let them
hear them.

30 And he said, Nay, father Abraham: but if one went unto them from the
dead, they will repent.

31 And he said unto him, If they hear not Moses and the prophets, neither
will they be persuaded, though one rose from the dead.

Chapter Seventeen

Offences

1 Then said he unto his disciples, It is impossible but that offences will come: but woe unto him, through whom they come!

2 It were better for him that a millstone were hanged about his neck, and he cast into the sea, than that he should offend one of these little ones.

3 Take heed to yourselves: If thy brother trespass against thee, rebuke him; and if he repent, forgive him.

4 And if he trespass against thee seven times in a day, and seven times in a day turn again to thee, saying, I repent; thou shalt forgive him.

Increase our Faith

5 And the apostles said unto the Lord, Increase our faith.

6 And the Lord said, If ye had faith as a grain of mustard seed, ye might say unto this sycamine tree, Be thou plucked up by the root, and be thou planted in the sea; and it should obey you.

7 But which of you, having a servant ploughing or feeding cattle, will say unto him by and by, when he is come from the field, Go and sit down to meat?

8 And will not rather say unto him, Make ready wherewith I may sup, and gird thyself, and serve me, till I have eaten and drunken; and afterward thou shalt eat and drink?

9 Doth he thank that servant because he did the things that were commanded him? I trow not.

10 So likewise ye, when ye shall have done all those things which are commanded you, say, We are unprofitable servants: we have done that which was our duty to do.

Where are the Nine?

11 And it came to pass, as he went to Jerusalem, that he passed through the midst of Samaria and Galilee.

12 And as he entered into a certain village, there met him ten men that
were lepers, which stood afar off:

13 And they lifted up their voices, and said, Jesus, Master, have mercy on
us.

14 And when he saw them, he said unto them, Go shew yourselves unto
the priests. And it came to pass, that, as they went, they were
cleansed.

15 And one of them, when he saw that he was healed, turned back, and
with a loud voice glorified God,

16 And fell down on his face at his feet, giving him thanks: And he was a
Samaritan.

17 And Jesus answering said, Were there not ten lepers cleansed? But
where are the nine?

18 There are not found that returned to give glory to God, save this
stranger.

19 And he said unto him, Arise, go thy way: thy faith hath made thee
whole.

The Coming of the Kingdom

20 And when he was demanded of the Pharisees, when the kingdom of
God should come, he answered them and said, The kingdom of God
cometh not with observation:

21 Neither shall they say, Lo here! Or, lo there! For, behold, the kingdom
of God is within you.

22 And he said unto the disciples, The days will come, when ye shall desire
to see one of the days of the Son of man, and ye shall not see it.

23 And they shall say to you, See here; or, see there: go not after them,
nor follow them.

24 For as the lightning, that lighteneth out of the one part under heaven,
shineth unto the other part under heaven; so shall also the Son of
man be in his day.

25 But first must he suffer many things, and be rejected of this generation.

26 And as it was in the days of Noe, so shall it be also in the days of the
Son of man.

27 They did eat, they drank, they married wives, they were given in
marriage, until the day that Noe entered into the ark, and the flood
came, and destroyed them all.

28 Likewise also as it was in the days of Lot; they did eat, they drank, they
bought, they sold, they planted, they builded;

29 But the same day that Lot went out of Sodom it rained fire and
brimstone from heaven, and destroyed them all.

30 Even thus shall it be in the day when the Son of man is revealed.

31 In that day, he which shall be upon the housetop, and his stuff in the
house, let him not come down to take it away: and he that is in the
field, let him likewise not return back.

32 Remember Lot's wife.

33 Whosoever shall seek to save his life shall lose it; and whosoever shall
lose his life shall preserve it.

34 I tell you, in that night there shall be two men in one bed; the one shall
be taken, and the other shall be left.

35 Two women shall be grinding together; the one shall be taken, and the
other left.

36 Two men shall be in the field; the one shall be taken, and the other left.

37 And they answered and said unto him, Where, Lord? And he said unto
them, Wheresoever the body is, thither will the eagles be gathered
together.

Chapter Eighteen

The Persistent Widow

1 And he spake a parable unto them to this end, that men ought always to
pray, and not to faint;

2 Saying, There was in a city a judge, which feared not God, neither
regarded man;

3 And there was a widow in that city; and she came unto him, saying,
Avenge me of mine adversary.

4 And he would not for a while; but afterward he said within himself,
Though I fear not God, nor regard man;

5 Yet because this widow troubleth me, I will avenge her, lest by her
continual coming she weary me.

6 And the Lord said, Hear what the unjust judge saith.

7 And shall not God avenge his own elect, which cry day and night unto
him, though he bear long with them?

8 I tell you that he will avenge them speedily. Nevertheless when the Son
of man cometh, shall he find faith on the earth?

The Pharisee and the Publican

9 And he spake this parable unto certain which trusted in themselves that
they were righteous, and despised others:

10 Two men went up into the temple to pray; the one a Pharisee and the
other a publican.

11 The Pharisee stood and prayed thus with himself, God, I thank thee,
that I am not as other men are, extortioners, unjust, adulterers, or
even as this publican.

12 I fast twice in the week, I give tithes of all that I possess.

13 And the publican, standing afar off, would not lift up so much as his eyes
unto heaven, but smote upon his breast, saying, God be merciful to
me a sinner.

14 I tell you, this man went down to his house justified rather than the
other: for everyone that exalteth himself shall be abased; and he that
humbleth himself shall be exalted.

Jesus Blesses Little Children

15 And they brought unto him also infants, that he would touch them: but
when his disciples saw it, they rebuked them.

16 But Jesus called them unto him, and said, Suffer little children to come
unto me, and forbid them not: for of such is the kingdom of God.

17 Verily I say unto you, Whosoever shall not receive the kingdom of God
as a little child shall in no wise enter therein.

The Rich Young Ruler

18 And a certain ruler asked him, saying, Good Master, what shall I do to
inherit eternal life?

19 And Jesus said unto him, Why callest thou me good? none is good, save one, that is, God.

20 Thou knowest the commandments, Do not commit adultery, Do not kill, Do not steal, Do not bear false witness, Honour thy father and thy mother.

21 And he said, All these have I kept from my youth up.

22 Now when Jesus heard these things, he said unto him, Yet lackest thou one thing: sell all that thou hast, and distribute unto the poor, and thou shalt have treasure in heaven: and come, follow me.

23 And when he heard this, he was very sorrowful: for he was very rich.

Who then can be Saved?

24 And when Jesus saw that he was very sorrowful, he said, How hardly shall they that have riches enter into the kingdom of God!

25 For it is easier for a camel to go through a needle's eye, than for a rich man to enter into the kingdom of God.

26 And they that heard it said, Who then can be saved?

27 And he said, The things which are impossible with men are possible with God.

28 Then Peter said, Lo, we have left all, and followed thee.

29 And he said unto them, Verily I say unto you, There is no man that hath left house, or parents, or brethren, or wife, or children, for the kingdom of God's sake,

30 Who shall not receive manifold more in this present time, and in the world to come life everlasting.

Jesus Predicts His Death and Resurrection

31 Then took he unto him the twelve, and said unto them, Behold, we go up to Jerusalem, and all things that are written by the prophets concerning the Son of man shall be accomplished.

32 For he shall be delivered unto the Gentiles, and shall be mocked, and spitefully entreated, and spitted on:

33 And they shall scourge him, and put him to death: and the third day he shall rise again.

34 And they understood none of these things: and this saying was hid from them, neither knew they the things which were spoken.

A Blind Beggar's Sight is Restored

35 And it came to pass, that as he was coming nigh unto Jericho, a certain blind man sat by the way side begging:

36 And hearing the multitude pass by, he asked what it meant.

37 And they told him, that Jesus of Nazareth passeth by.

38 And he cried, saying, Jesus, thou Son of David, have mercy on me.

39 And they which went before rebuked him, that he should hold his peace: but he cried so much the more, Thou Son of David, have mercy on me.

40 And Jesus stood, and commanded him to be brought unto him: and when he was come near, he asked him,

41 Saying, What wilt thou that I shall do unto thee? And he said, Lord, that I may receive my sight.

42 And Jesus said unto him, Receive thy sight: thy faith hath saved thee.

43 And immediately he received his sight, and followed him, glorifying God: and all the people, when they saw it, gave praise unto God.

Chapter Nineteen

'This Day is Salvation come to this House'

1 And Jesus entered and passed through Jericho.

2 And, behold, there was a man named Zacchaeus, which was the chief among the publicans, and he was rich.

3 And he sought to see Jesus who he was; and could not for the press, because he was little of stature.

4 And he ran before, and climbed up into a sycomore tree to see him: for he was to pass that way.

5 And when Jesus came to the place, he looked up, and saw him, and said unto him, Zacchaeus, make haste, and come down; for today I must abide at thy house.

6 And he made haste, and came down, and received him joyfully.

7 And when they saw it, they all murmured, saying, That he was gone to
be guest with a man that is a sinner.

8 And Zacchaeus stood, and said unto the Lord; Behold, Lord, the half of
my goods I give to the poor; and if I have taken any thing from any
man by false accusation, I restore him fourfold.

9 And Jesus said unto him, This day is salvation come to this house,
forasmuch as he also is a son of Abraham.

10 For the Son of man is come to seek and to save that which was lost.

Ten Pounds

11 And as they heard these things, he added and spake a parable, because
he was nigh to Jerusalem, and because they thought that the kingdom
of God should immediately appear.

12 He said therefore, A certain nobleman went into a far country to
receive for himself a kingdom, and to return.

13 And he called his ten servants, and delivered them ten pounds, and said
unto them, Occupy till I come.

14 But his citizens hated him, and sent a message after him, saying, We will
not have this man to reign over us.

15 And it came to pass, that when he was returned, having received the
kingdom, then he commanded these servants to be called unto him,
to whom he had given the money, that he might know how much
every man had gained by trading.

16 Then came the first, saying, Lord, thy pound hath gained ten pounds.

17 And he said unto him, Well, thou good servant: because thou hast been
faithful in a very little, have thou authority over ten cities.

18 And the second came, saying, Lord, thy pound hath gained five pounds.

19 And he said likewise to him, Be thou also over five cities.

20 And another came, saying, Lord, behold, here is thy pound, which I
have kept laid up in a napkin:

21 For I feared thee, because thou art an austere man: thou takest up that
thou layest not down, and reapest that thou didst not sow.

22 And he saith unto him, Out of thine own mouth will I judge thee, thou
wicked servant. Thou knewest that I was an austere man, taking up
that I laid not down, and reaping that I did not sow:

23 Wherefore then gavest not thou my money into the bank, that at my coming I might have required mine own with usury?

24 And he said unto them that stood by, Take from him the pound, and give it to him that hath ten pounds.

25 (And they said unto him, Lord, he hath ten pounds.)

26 For I say unto you, that unto every one which hath shall be given; and from him that hath not, even that he hath shall be taken away from him.

27 But those mine enemies, which would not that I should reign over them, bring hither, and slay them before me.

The Triumphal Entry

28 And when he had thus spoken, he went before, ascending up to Jerusalem.

29 And it came to pass, when he was come nigh to Bethphage and Bethany, at the mount called the mount of Olives, he sent two of his disciples,

30 Saying, Go ye into the village over against you; in the which at your entering ye shall find a colt tied, whereon yet never man sat: loose him, and bring him hither.

31 And if any man ask you, Why do ye loose him? Thus shall ye say unto him, Because the Lord hath need of him.

32 And they that were sent went their way, and found even as he had said unto them.

33 And as they were loosing the colt, the owners thereof said unto them, Why loose ye the colt?

34 And they said, The Lord hath need of him.

35 And they brought him to Jesus: and they cast their garments upon the colt, and they set Jesus thereon.

36 And as he went, they spread their clothes in the way.

37 And when he was come nigh, even now at the descent of the mount of Olives, the whole multitude of the disciples began to rejoice and praise God with a loud voice for all the mighty works that they had seen;

38 Saying, Blessed be the King that cometh in the name of the Lord: peace in heaven, and glory in the highest.

39 And some of the Pharisees from among the multitude said unto him, Master, rebuke thy disciples.

40 And he answered and said unto them, I tell you that, if these should hold their peace, the stones would immediately cry out.

Jesus Weeps over Jerusalem

41 And when he was come near, he beheld the city, and wept over it.

42 Saying, If thou hadst known, even thou, at least in this thy day, the things which belong unto thy peace! But now they are hid from thine eyes.

43 For the days shall come upon thee, that thine enemies shall cast a trench about thee, and compass thee round, and keep thee in on every side.

44 And shall lay thee even with the ground, and thy children within thee; and they shall not leave in thee one stone upon another; because thou knewest not the time of thy visitation.

'My House is the House of Prayer'

45 And he went into the temple, and began to cast out them that sold therein, and them that bought;

46 Saying unto them, It is written, My house is the house of prayer: but ye have made it a den of thieves.

47 And he taught daily in the temple. But the chief priests and the scribes and the chief of the people sought to destroy him.

48 And could not find what they might do: for all the people were very attentive to hear him.

Chapter Twenty

Christ's Authority is Challenged

1 And it came to pass, that on one of those days, as he taught the people in the temple, and preached the gospel, the chief priests and the scribes came upon him with the elders.

2 And spake unto him, saying, Tell us, by what authority doest thou these things? Or who is he that gave thee this authority?

3 And he answered and said unto them, I will also ask you one thing; and answer me:

4 The baptism of John, was it from heaven, or of men?

5 And they reasoned with themselves, saying, If we shall say, From heaven; he will say, Why then believed ye him not?

6 But and if we say, Of men; all the people will stone us: for they be persuaded that John was a prophet.

7 And they answered, that they could not tell whence it was.

8 And Jesus said unto them, Neither tell I you by what authority I do these things.

The Wicked Husbandmen

9 Then began he to speak to the people this parable; A certain man planted a vineyard, and let it forth to husbandmen, and went into a far country for a long time.

10 And at the season he sent a servant to the husbandmen, that they should give him of the fruit of the vineyard: but the husbandmen beat him, and sent him away empty.

11 And again he sent another servant: and they beat him also, and entreated him shamefully, and sent him away empty.

12 And again he sent a third: and they wounded him also, and cast him out.

13 Then said the lord of the vineyard, What shall I do? I will send my beloved son: it may be they will reverence him when they see him.

14 But when the husbandmen saw him, they reasoned among themselves, saying, This is the heir: come, let us kill him, that the inheritance may be ours.

15 So they cast him out of the vineyard, and killed him. What therefore shall the lord of the vineyard do unto them?

16 He shall come and destroy these husbandmen, and shall give the vineyard to others. And when they heard it, they said, God forbid.

17 And he beheld them, and said, What is this then that is written, The stone which the builders rejected, the same is become the head of the corner?

18 Whosoever shall fall upon that stone shall be broken; but on whomsoever it shall fall, it will grind him to powder.

19 And the chief priests and the scribes the same hour sought to lay hands on him; and they feared the people: for they perceived that he had spoken this parable against them.

A Penny

20 And they watched him, and sent forth spies, which should feign themselves just men, that they might take hold of his words, that so they might deliver him unto the power and authority of the governor.

21 And they asked him, saying, Master, we know that thou sayest and teachest rightly, neither acceptest thou the person of any, but teachest the way of God truly:

22 Is it lawful for us to give tribute unto Caesar, or no?

23 But he perceived their craftiness, and said unto them, Why tempt ye me?

24 Shew me a penny. Whose image and superscription hath it? They answered and said, Caesar's.

25 And he said unto them, Render therefore unto Caesar the things which be Caesar's, and unto God the things which be God's.

26 And they could not take hold of his words before the people: and they marvelled at his answer, and held their peace.

Widowed Seven Times

27 Then came to him certain of the Sadducees, which deny that there is any resurrection; and they asked him,

28 Saying, Master, Moses wrote unto us, If any man's brother die, having a wife, and he die without children, that his brother should take his wife, and raise up seed unto his brother.

29 There were therefore seven brethren: and the first took a wife, and died without children.

30 And the second took her to wife, and he died childless.

31 And the third took her; and in like manner the seven also: and they left no children, and died.

32 Last of all the woman died also.

33 Therefore in the resurrection whose wife of them is she? For seven had her to wife.

34 And Jesus answering said unto them, The children of this world marry, and are given in marriage:

35 But they which shall be accounted worthy to attain that world, and the resurrection from the dead, neither marry, nor are given in marriage:

36 Neither can they die any more: for they are equal unto the angels; and are the children of God, being the children of the resurrection.

37 Now that the dead are raised, even Moses shewed at the bush, when he calleth the Lord the God of Abraham, and the God of Isaac, and the God of Jacob.

38 For he is not a God of the dead, but of the living: for all live unto him.

39 Then certain of the scribes answering said, Master, thou hast well said.

40 And after that they durst not ask him any question at all.

Jesus puts a Question to the Scribes

41 And he said unto them, How say they that Christ is David's son?

42 And David himself saith in the book of Psalms, the Lord said unto my Lord, Sit thou on my right hand,

43 Till I make thine enemies thy footstool.

44 David therefore calleth him Lord, how is he then his son?

45 Then in the audience of all the people he said unto his disciples,

46 Beware of the scribes, which desire to walk in long robes, and love greetings in the markets, and the highest seats in the synagogues, and the chief rooms at feasts;

47 Which devour widows' houses, and for a shew make long prayers: the same shall receive greater damnation.

Chapter Twenty One

A Widow's Offering

1 And he looked up, and saw the rich men casting their gifts into the treasury.

2 And he saw also a certain poor widow casting in thither two mites.

3 And he said, Of a truth I say unto you, that this poor widow hath cast in more than they all:

4 For all these have of their abundance cast in unto the offering of God: but she of her penury hath cast in all the living that she had.

The Destruction of the Temple Predicted

5 And as some spake of the temple, how it was adorned with goodly stones and gifts, he said,

6 As for these things which ye behold, the days will come, in the which there shall not be left one stone upon another, that shall not be thrown down.

Signs

7 And they asked him, saying, Master, but when shall these things be? And what sign will there be when these things shall come to pass?

8 And he said, Take heed that ye be not deceived: for many shall come in my name, saying, I am Christ; and the time draweth near: go ye not therefore after them.

9 But when ye shall hear of wars and commotions, be not terrified: for these things must first come to pass: but the end is not by and by.

10 Then said he unto them, Nation shall rise against nation, and kingdom against kingdom:

11And great earthquakes shall be in divers places, and famines, and pestilences; and fearful sights and great signs shall there be from heaven.

12 But before all these, they shall lay their hands on you, and persecute you, delivering you up to the synagogues, and into prisons, being brought before kings and rulers for my name's sake.

13 And it shall turn to you for a testimony.

14 Settle it therefore in your hearts, not to meditate before what ye shall answer:

15 For I will give you a mouth and wisdom, which all your adversaries shall not be able to gainsay nor resist.

16 And ye shall be betrayed both by parents, and brethren, and kinsfolks, and friend; and some of you shall they cause to be put to death.

17 And ye shall be hated of all men for my name's sake.

18 But there shall not an hair of your head perish.

19 In your patience possess ye your souls.

The Destruction of Jerusalem Foretold

20 And when ye shall see Jerusalem compassed with armies, then know that the desolation thereof is nigh.

21 Then let them which are in Judaea flee to the mountains; and let them which are in the midst of it depart out; and let not them that are in the countries enter thereinto.

22 For these be the days of vengeance, that all things which are written may be fulfilled.

23 But woe unto them that are with child, and to them that give suck, in those days! For there shall be great distress in the land, and wrath upon this people.

24 And they shall fall by the edge of the sword, and shall be led away captive into all nations: and Jerusalem shall be trodden down of the Gentiles, until the times of the Gentiles be fulfilled.

Signs Preceding the Second Coming of Christ

25 And there shall be signs in the sun, and in the moon, and in the stars; and upon the earth distress of nations, with perplexity; the sea and the waves roaring;

26 Men's hearts failing them for fear, and for looking after those things which are coming on the earth: for the powers of heaven shall be shaken.

27 And then shall they see the Son of man coming in a cloud with power and great glory.

28 And when these things begin to come to pass, then look up, and lift up your heads; for your redemption draweth nigh.

The Fig Tree

29 And he spake to them a parable: Behold the fig tree, and all the trees;

30 When they now shoot forth, ye see and know of your own selves that summer is now nigh at hand.

31 So likewise ye, when ye see these things come to pass, know ye that the kingdom of God is nigh at hand.

32 Verily I say unto you, This generation shall not pass away, till all be fulfilled.

33 Heaven and earth shall pass away: but my words shall not pass away.

Watch Ye Therefore

34 And take heed to yourselves, lest at any time your hearts be overcharged with surfeiting, and drunkenness, and cares of this life, and so that day come upon you unawares.

35 For as a snare shall it come on all them that dwell on the face of the whole earth.

36 Watch ye therefore, and pray always, that ye may be accounted worthy to escape all these things that shall come to pass, and to stand before the Son of man.

37 And in the day time he was teaching in the temple; and at night he went out, and abode in the mount that is called the mount of Olives.

38 And all the people came early in the morning to him in the temple, for to hear him.

Chapter Twenty Two

Judas Plots to Betray Jesus

1 Now the feast of unleavened bread drew nigh, which is called the Passover.

2 And the chief priests and scribes sought how they might kill him; for they feared the people.

3 Then entered Satan into Judas surnamed Iscariot, being of the number of the twelve.

4 And he went his way, and communed with the chief priests and captains, how he might betray him unto them.

5 And they were glad, and covenanted to give him money.

6 And he promised, and sought opportunity to betray him unto them in the absence of the multitude.

The Last Supper

7 Then came the day of unleavened bread, when the passover must be killed.

8 And he sent Peter and John, saying, Go and prepare us the passover, that we may eat.

9 And they said unto him, Where wilt thou that we prepare?

10 And he said unto them, Behold, when ye are entered into the city, there shall a man meet you, bearing a pitcher of water; follow him into the house where he entereth in.

11 And ye shall say unto the goodman of the house, The Master saith unto thee, Where is the guest-chamber, where I shall eat the passover with my disciples?

12 And he shall shew you a large upper room furnished: there make ready.

13 And they went, and found as he had said unto them: and they made ready the passover.

14 And when the hour was come, he sat down, and the twelve apostles with him.

15 And he said unto them, With desire I have desired to eat this passover with you before I suffer:

16 For I say unto you, I will not any more eat thereof, until it be fulfilled in the kingdom of God.

17 And he took the cup, and gave thanks, and said, Take this, and divide it among yourselves:

18 For I say unto you, I will not drink of the fruit of the vine, until the kingdom of God shall come.

19 And he took bread, and gave thanks, and brake it, and gave unto them, saying, This is my body which is given for you: this do in remembrance of me.

20 Likewise also the cup after supper, saying, This cup is the new testament in my blood, which is shed for you.

21 But, behold, the hand of him that betrayeth me is with me on the table.

22 And truly the Son of man goeth, as it was determined: but woe unto that man by whom he is betrayed!

23 And they began to inquire among themselves, which of them it was that should do this thing.

24 And there was also a strife among them, which of them should be accounted the greatest.

25 And he said unto them, The kings of the Gentiles exercise lordship over them; and they that exercise authority upon them are called benefactors.

26 But ye shall not be so: but he that is greatest among you, let him be as the younger; and he that is chief, as he that doth serve.

27 For whether is greater, he that sitteth at meat, or he that serveth? is not he that sitteth at meat? But I am among you as he that serveth.

28 Ye are they which have continued with me in my temptations.

29 And I appoint unto you a kingdom, as my Father hath appointed unto me;

30 That ye may eat and drink at my table in my kingdom, and sit on thrones judging the twelve tribes of Israel.

31 And the Lord said, Simon, Simon, behold, Satan hath desired to have you, that he may sift you as wheat:

32 But I have prayed for thee, that thy faith fail not: and when thou art converted, strengthen thy brethren.

33 And he said unto him, Lord, I am ready to go with thee, both into prison, and to death.

34 And he said, I tell thee, Peter, the cock shall not crow this day, before thou shalt thrice deny that thou knowest me.

35 And he said unto them, When I sent you without purse, and scrip, and shoes, lacked ye any thing? And they said, Nothing.

36 Then said he unto them, But now he that hath a purse, let him take it, and likewise his scrip: and he that hath no sword, let him sell his garment, and buy one.

37 For I say unto you, that this that is written must yet be accomplished in me, And he was reckoned among the transgressors: for the things concerning me have an end.

38 And they said, Lord, behold, here are two swords. And he said unto them, It is enough.

Jesus Prays in the Garden of Gethsemane

39 And he came out, and went, as he was wont, to the mount of Olives; and his disciples also followed him.

40 And when he was at the place, he said unto them, Pray that ye enter not into temptation.

41 And he was withdrawn from them about a stone's cast, and kneeled down, and prayed,

42 Saying, Father, if thou be willing, remove this cup from me: nevertheless not my will, but thine, be done.

43 And there appeared an angel unto him from heaven, strengthening him.

44 And being in an agony he prayed more earnestly: and his sweat was as it were great drops of blood falling down to the ground.

45 And when he rose up from prayer, and was come to his disciples, he found them sleeping for sorrow,

46 And said unto them, Why sleep ye? rise and pray, lest ye enter into temptation.

Betrayed with a Kiss

47 And while he yet spake, behold a multitude, and he that was called Judas, one of the twelve, went before them, and drew near unto Jesus to kiss him.

48 But Jesus said unto him, Judas, betrayest thou the Son of man with a kiss?

49 When they which were about him saw what would follow, they said unto him, Lord, shall we smite with the sword?

50 And one of them smote the servant of the high priest, and cut off his right ear.

51 And Jesus answered and said, suffer ye thus far. And he touched his ear, and healed him.

52 Then Jesus said unto the chief priests, and captains of the temple, and the elders, which were come to him, Be ye come out, as against a thief, with swords and staves?

53 When I was daily with you in the temple, ye stretched forth no hands against me: but this is your hour, and the power of darkness.

Peter Denies Jesus

54 Then took they him, and led him, and brought him into the high priest's house. And Peter followed afar off.

55 And when they had kindled a fire in the midst of the hall, and were set down together, Peter sat down among them.

56 But a certain maid beheld him as he sat by the fire, and earnestly looked upon him, and said, This man was also with him.

57 And he denied him, saying, Woman, I know him not.

58 And after a little while another saw him, and said, Thou art also of them. And Peter said, Man, I am not.

59 And about the space of one hour after another confidently affirmed, saying, Of a truth this fellow also was with him: for he is a Galilaean.

60 And Peter said, Man, I know not what thou sayest. And immediately, while he yet spake, the cock crew.

61 And the Lord turned, and looked upon Peter. And Peter remembered the word of the Lord, how he had said unto him, Before the cock crow, thou shalt deny me thrice.

62 And Peter went out, and wept bitterly.

Jesus is Mocked and Beaten

63 And the men that held Jesus mocked him, and smote him.

64 And when they had blindfolded him, they struck him on the face, and asked him, saying, Prophesy, who is it that smote thee?

65 And many other things blasphemously spake they against him.

Jesus before the Jewish Council

66 And as soon as it was day, the elders of the people and the chief priests and the scribes came together, and led him into their council, saying,

67 Art thou the Christ? tell us. And he said unto them, If I tell you, ye will not believe.

68 And if I also ask you, ye will not answer me, nor let me go.

69 Hereafter shall the Son of man sit on the right hand of the power of God.

70 Then said they all, Art thou the Son of God? And he said unto them, Ye say that I am.

71 And they said, What need we any further witness? For we ourselves have heard of his own mouth.

Chapter Twenty Three

Jesus is Taken to Pilate and Herod

1 And the whole multitude of them arose, and led him unto Pilate.

2 And they began to accuse him, saying, We found this fellow perverting the nation, and forbidding to give tribute to Caesar, saying that he himself is Christ a King.

3 And Pilate asked him, saying, Art thou the King of the Jews? And he answered him and said, Thou sayest it.

4 Then said Pilate to the chief priests and to the people, I find no fault in this man.

5 And they were the more fierce, saying, he stirreth up the people, teaching throughout all Jewry, beginning from Galilee to this place.

6 When Pilate heard of Galilee, he asked whether the man were a Galilaean.

7 And as soon as he knew that he belonged unto Herod's jurisdiction, he sent him to Herod, who himself also was at Jerusalem at that time.

8 And when Herod saw Jesus, he was exceeding glad: for he was desirous to see him of a long season, because he had heard many things of him; and he hoped to have seen some miracle done by him.

9 Then he questioned with him in many words; but he answered him nothing.

10 And the chief priests and scribes stood and vehemently accused him.

11 And Herod with his men of war set him at nought, and mocked him, and arrayed him in a gorgeous robe, and sent him again to Pilate.

12 And the same day Pilate and Herod were made friends together: for before they were at enmity between themselves.

A Murderer is Released, but Jesus is Condemned

13 And Pilate, when he had called together the chief priests and the rulers of the people,

14 Said unto them, Ye have brought this man unto me, as one that perverteth the people: and, behold, I, having examined him before you, have found no fault in this man touching those things whereof ye accuse him:

15 No, nor yet Herod: for I sent you to him; and, lo, nothing worthy of death is done unto him.

16 I will therefore chastise him, and release him.

17 (For of necessity he must release one unto them at the feast.)

18 And they cried out all at once, saying, Away with this man, and release unto us Barabbas:

19 (Who for a certain sedition made in the city, and for murder, was cast into prison.)

20 Pilate therefore, willing to release Jesus, spake again to them.

21 But they cried, saying, Crucify him, crucify him.

22 And he said unto them the third time, Why, what evil hath he done? I have found no cause of death in him: I will therefore chastise him, and let him go.

23 And they were instant with loud voices, requiring that he might be crucified. And the voices of them and of the chief priests prevailed.

24 And Pilate gave sentence that it should be as they required.

25 And he released unto them him that for sedition and murder was cast into prison, whom they had desired: but he delivered Jesus to their will.

A King is Crucified

26 And as they led him away, they laid hold upon one Simon, a Cyrenian, coming out of the country, and on him they laid the cross, that he might bear it after Jesus.

27 And there followed him a great company of people, and of women, which also bewailed and lamented him.

28 But Jesus turning unto them said, Daughters of Jerusalem, weep not for me, but weep for yourselves, and for your children.

29 For, behold, the days are coming, in the which they shall say, Blessed are the barren, and the wombs that never bare, and the paps which never gave suck.

30 Then shall they begin to say to the mountains, Fall on us; and to the hills, Cover us.

31 For if they do these things in a green tree, what shall be done in the dry?

32 And there were also two other, malefactors, led with him to be put to death.

33 And when they were come to the place, which is called Calvary, there they crucified him, and the malefactors, one on the right hand, and the other on the left.

34 Then said Jesus, Father, forgive them; for they know not what they do. And they parted his raiment, and cast lots.

35 And the people stood beholding. And the rulers also with them derided him, saying, He saved others; let him save himself, if he be Christ, the chosen of God.

36 And the soldiers also mocked him, coming to him, and offering him vinegar.

37 And saying, If thou be the king of the Jews, save thyself.

38 And a superscription also was written over him in letters of Greek, and Latin, and Hebrew, THIS IS THE KING OF THE JEWS.

39 And one of the malefactors which were hanged railed on him, saying, If thou be Christ, save thyself and us.

40 But the other answering rebuked him, saying, Dost not thou fear God, seeing thou art in the same condemnation?

41 And we indeed justly; for we receive the due reward of our deeds: but this man hath done nothing amiss.

42 And he said unto Jesus, Lord, remember me when thou comest into thy kingdom.

43 And Jesus said unto him, Verily I say unto thee, Today shalt thou be with me in paradise.

The Death of Christ

44 And it was about the sixth hour, and there was a darkness over all the earth until the ninth hour.

45 And the sun was darkened, and the veil of the temple was rent in the midst.

46 And when Jesus had cried with a loud voice, he said, Father, into thy hands I commend my spirit: and having said thus, he gave up the ghost.

47 Now when the centurion saw what was done, he glorified God, saying, Certainly this was a righteous man.

48 And all the people that came together to that sight, beholding the things which were done, smote their breasts, and returned.

49 And all his acquaintance, and the women that followed him from Galilee, stood afar off, beholding these things.

Jesus is Buried

50 And, behold, there was a man named Joseph, a counsellor; and he was a good man, and a just:

51 (The same had not consented to the counsel and deed of them;) he was of Arimathaea, a city of the Jews: who also himself waited for the kingdom of God.

52 This man went unto Pilate, and begged the body of Jesus.

53 And he took it down, and wrapped it in linen, and laid it in a sepulchre that was hewn in stone, wherein never man before was laid.

54 And that day was the preparation, and the sabbath drew on.

55 And the women also, which came with him from Galilee, followed after, and beheld the sepulchre, and how his body was laid.

56 And they returned, and prepared spices and ointments; and rested the sabbath day according to the commandment.

Chapter Twenty Four

Christ's Resurrection

1 Now upon the first day of the week, very early in the morning, they came unto the sepulchre, bringing the spices which they had prepared, and certain others with them.

2 And they found the stone rolled away from the sepulchre.

3 And they entered in, and found not the body of the Lord Jesus.

4 And it came to pass, as they were much perplexed thereabout, behold, two men stood by them in shining garments:

5 And as they were afraid, and bowed down their faces to the earth, they said unto them, Why seek ye the living among the dead?

6 He is not here, but is risen: remember how he spake unto you when he was yet in Galilee,

7 Saying, The Son of man must be delivered into the hands of sinful men, and be crucified, and the third day rise again.

8 And they remembered his words,

9 And returned from the sepulchre, and told all these things unto the eleven, and to all the rest.

10 It was Mary Magdalene, and Joanna, and Mary the mother of James, and other women that were with them, which told these things unto the apostles.

11 And their words seemed to them as idle tales, and they believed them not.

12 Then arose Peter, and ran unto the sepulchre; and stooping down, he beheld the linen clothes laid by themselves, and departed, wondering in himself at that which was come to pass.

On the Road to Emmaus

13 And behold, two of them went that same day to a village called
   Emmaus, which was from Jerusalem about threescore furlongs.

14 And they talked together of all these things which had happened.

15 And it came to pass, that, while they communed together and
   reasoned, Jesus himself drew near, and went with them.

16 But their eyes were holden that they should not know him.

17 And he said unto them, What manner of communications are these
   that ye have one to another, as ye walk, and are sad?

18 And one of them, whose name was Cleopas, answering said unto him,
   Art thou only a stranger in Jerusalem, and hast not known the things
   which are come to pass there in these days?

19 And he said unto them, What things? And they said unto him,
   Concerning Jesus of Nazareth, which was a prophet mighty in deed
   and word before God and all the people:

20 And how the chief priests and our rulers delivered him to be
   condemned to death, and have crucified him.

21 But we trusted that it had been he which should have redeemed Israel:
   and beside all this, today is the third day since these things were
   done.

22 Yea, and certain women also of our company made us astonished,
   which were early at the sepulchre:

23 And when they found not his body, they came, saying, that they had
   also seen a vision of angels, which said that he was alive.

24 And certain of them which were with us went to the sepulchre, and
   found it even so as the women had said: but him they saw not.

25 Then he said unto them, O fools, and slow of heart to believe all that
   the prophets have spoken:

26 Ought not Christ to have suffered these things, and to enter into his
   glory?

27 And beginning at Moses and all the prophets, he expounded unto them
   in all the scriptures the things concerning himself.

The Disciples' Eyes are Opened

28 And they drew nigh unto the village, whither they went: and he made as
    though he would have gone further.
29 But they constrained him, saying, Abide with us: for it is toward evening,
    and the day is far spent. And he went in to tarry with them.
30 And it came to pass, as he sat at meat with them, he took bread, and
    blessed it, and brake, and gave to them.
31 And their eyes were opened, and they knew him; and he vanished out
    of their sight.
32 And they said one to another, Did not our heart burn within us, while
    he talked with us by the way, and while he opened to us the
    scriptures?
33 And they rose up the same hour, and returned to Jerusalem, and found
    the eleven gathered together, and them that were with them,
34 Saying, The Lord is risen indeed, and hath appeared to Simon.
35 And they told what things were done in the way, and how he was
    known of them in breaking of bread.

Jesus Appears to His Disciples

36 And as they thus spake, Jesus himself stood in the midst of them, and
    saith unto them, Peace be unto you.
37 But they were terrified and affrighted, and supposed that they had seen
    a spirit.
38 And he said unto them, Why are ye troubled? and why do thoughts
    arise in your hearts?
39 Behold my hands and my feet, that it is I myself: handle me, and see; for
    a spirit hath not flesh and bones, as ye see me have.
40 And when he had thus spoken, he shewed them his hands and his feet.
41 And while they yet believed not for joy, and wondered, he said unto
    them, Have ye here any meat?
42 And they gave him a piece of a broiled fish, and of an honeycomb.
43 And he took it, and did eat before them.
44 And he said unto them, These are the words which I spake unto you,
    while I was yet with you, that all things must be fulfilled, which were
    written in the law of Moses, and in the prophets, concerning me.

45 Then opened he their understanding, that they might understand the scriptures.

46 And said unto them, Thus it is written, and thus it behoved Christ to suffer, and to rise from the dead the third day:

47 And that repentance and remission of sins should be preached in his name among all nations, beginning at Jerusalem.

48 And ye are witnesses of these things.

49 And behold, I send the promise of my Father upon you: but tarry ye in the city of Jerusalem, until ye be endued with power from on high.

The Ascension of Christ into Heaven

50 And he led them out as far as to Bethany, and he lifted up his hands, and blessed them.

51 And it came to pass, while he blessed them, he was parted from them, and carried up into heaven.

52 And they worshipped him, and returned to Jerusalem with great joy:

53 And were continually in the temple, praising and blessing God. Amen.

Scripture References for New Life in Luke

Introduction

1: Luke Ch.8 v. 25
2: John Ch.8 v. 32
3: Luke Ch.8 v. 25
4: Romans Ch.3 v. 10
5: Romans Ch.3 v. 23

6: Acts Ch.4 v. 12
7: Isaiah Ch.55 v. 6
8: 2 Corinthians Ch.6 v. 2
9: Revelation Ch.3 v. 20

Lesson 1
Background to the Gospel of Luke

1: Colossians Ch.4 v. 14
2: Jeremiah Ch.33 v. 6
3: Jeremiah Ch.33 v. 8
4: Acts Ch.16 vs. 9, 10
5: Romans Ch.3 v. 23
6: Romans Ch.6 v. 23
7: Matthew Ch.18 v. 9
8: Matthew Ch.25 v. 41
9: Matthew Ch.25 v. 46
10: 2 Timothy Ch.3 v. 15

11: Romans Ch.3 v. 10
12: Revelation Ch.21 v.8
13: Mark Ch.1 v. 15
14: Ecclesiastes Ch.7 v. 20
15: 1 John Ch.1 v. 9
16: Luke Ch.13 v. 3
17: Isaiah Ch.1 v. 18
18: Isaiah Ch.55 v. 7
19: Romans Ch.6 v. 23

Lesson 2
The Angel visits Mary

1: Luke Ch.1 v. 38
2: Matthew Ch.1 v. 20
3: 1 John Ch.1 v. 8
4: Isaiah Ch.64 v. 6
5: Romans Ch.5 v. 12
6: Revelation Ch.21 v. 8
7: John Ch.14 v. 6

8: John Ch.5 v. 24
9: Matthew Ch.23 v. 33
10: Hebrews Ch.2 v. 3
11: Acts Ch.3 v. 19
12: Hebrews Ch.13 v. 5
13: Hebrews Ch.13 v. 6

Lesson 3
The Conception of Jesus

1: Luke Ch.1 v. 35
2: Hebrews Ch.7 v. 26
3: Hebrews Ch.4 v. 15
4: 1 Peter Ch.1 v. 19
5: 1 Peter Ch.2 vs. 22, 23
6: Isaiah Ch.53 v. 7
7: John Ch.1 v. 29
8: 1 John Ch.3 v. 5

9: Luke Ch.1 vs. 32, 35
10: Matthew Ch.1 v. 23
11: Isaiah Ch.9 v. 6
12: Galatians Ch.4 vs. 4, 5
13: John Ch.1 v. 14
14: Philippians Ch.2 vs. 7, 8
15: Acts Ch.4 v. 12

Lesson 4
The Birth of Jesus

1: Galatians Ch.4 v. 4
2: Luke Ch.2 v. 7
3: 2 Corinthians Ch.8 v. 9
4: Revelation Ch.3 v. 20

5: Genesis Ch.6 v.3
6: Hebrews Ch.3 v. 15
7: 1 John Ch.5 vs. 11, 12

Lesson 5
The Child Jesus in the Temple

1: Matthew Ch.1 v. 21
2: Isaiah Ch.7 v. 14
3: Isaiah Ch.9 vs. 6, 7
4: 1 John Ch.5 v. 11
5: Luke Ch.2 vs. 30, 31
6: Romans Ch.6 v. 23

7: Isaiah Ch.42 v. 7
8: 1 Timothy Ch.1 v. 15
9: Mark Ch.16 v. 15
10: Acts Ch.13 v. 47
11: Revelation Ch.5 v. 9
12: Isaiah Ch.45 v. 22

Lesson 6
Christ is Greater than the Prophets and Angels

1: Hebrews Ch.3 v. 3
2: Hebrews Ch.1 vs. 1 – 3
3: John Ch. 1 v. 3
4: Colossians Ch. 1 vs. 16, 17
5: Hebrews Ch.1 vs. 1 – 3
6: Hebrews Ch.1 vs. 4 - 6, 8, 10, 13
7: John Ch. 3 v. 3

8: John Ch.3 vs. 5 – 7
9: Titus Ch.3 vs. 5, 6
10: Luke Ch.3 v. 16
11: Acts Ch.4 v. 12
12: 1 John Ch.5 v. 11
13: Jeremiah Ch.33 v. 3

Lesson 7
The Saviour Identifies with Sinners

1: 1 John Ch.3 v. 5
2: 1 Peter Ch.1 v.19
3: 1 Peter Ch.2 v. 22
4: Hebrews Ch.4 v. 15
5: Hebrews Ch.7 v. 26
6: Isaiah Ch.53 vs. 4- 6
7: Romans Ch.5 v. 8
8: John Ch.1 v. 32

9: Matthew Ch.3 v. 17
10: John Ch.1 v. 34
11: Matthew Ch. 9 vs. 10, 11
12: Matthew Ch.9 v. 13
13: Luke Ch.7 v. 47
14: Luke Ch.15 vs. 1, 2
15: Luke Ch.19 v. 10
16: Isaiah Ch.1 v. 18
17: John Ch. 6 v. 37

Lesson 8
Jesus Shows His Power

1: Luke Ch.4 v. 34
2: Luke Ch.4 v. 36
3: John Ch.11 vs. 43, 44
4: John Ch.10 vs. 17, 18
5: Revelation Ch.1 v. 18
6: Luke Ch.8 v. 25
7: Matthew Ch.14 vs. 22 – 25

8: John Ch.2 vs. 1 – 11
9: Luke Ch.5 v. 21
10: Luke Ch.7 v. 16
11: 1 John Ch.1 v. 8
12: 1 John Ch.1 v. 10
13: 1 John Ch.1 v. 9

Lesson 9
Christ's Mission

1: Matthew Ch.1 vs. 20, 21
2: Luke Ch.19 v. 10
3: John Ch.3 v. 17
4: John Ch.12 v. 47
5: Matthew Ch.20 v. 28
6: John Ch.9 v. 5

7: 2 Corinthians Ch.4 vs. 3, 4
8: Matthew Ch.5 v. 17
9: John Ch.18 v. 37
10: Luke Ch.4 v. 43
11: 1 Timothy Ch.1 v. 15
12: Galatians Ch.2 v. 20

Lesson 10
The Parables of Jesus

1: Luke Ch.15 v. 10
2: Romans Ch. 3 v. 23
3: Proverbs Ch.20 v. 9
4: Romans Ch.3 v. 10
5: Isaiah Ch.53 v. 6
6: Luke Ch.13 v. 3
7: John Ch.6 v. 37
8: Psalm 32 v. 5
9: 1 John Ch.1 v. 9

10: Isaiah Ch.1 v. 18
11: Isaiah Ch.55 v. 7
12: Psalm 103 vs. 8 – 13
13: 2 Peter Ch.3 v. 9
14: Luke Ch.19 v. 10
15: Isaiah Ch.55 v. 6
16: 2 Corinthians Ch.6 v. 2
17: Jeremiah Ch.29 v. 13

Lesson 11
Jesus is Forsaken

1: Isaiah Ch.53 v. 3
2: Matthew Ch. 26 v. 56
3: Matthew Ch.27 v. 46
4: 1 Peter Ch. 2 v. 24
5: Isaiah Ch.53 v. 5
6: Isaiah Ch.53 v. 6

7: Hebrews Ch.9 v. 22
8: John Ch.14 v. 6
9: 1 John Ch.1 v. 7
10: Romans Ch. 5 v. 9
11: Ephesians Ch. 1 vs. 6, 7
12: Revelation Ch. 1 v. 5

Lesson 12
The Resurrection of Jesus Christ

1: Romans Ch. 1 vs. 3, 4
2: 1 Corinthians Ch. 15 vs. 3 – 8
3: 1 Corinthians Ch. 15 vs. 17, 18
4: 1 Corinthians Ch. 15 vs. 20 – 22
5: 2 Corinthians Ch. 4 v. 14
6: John Ch. 5 v. 29
7: Romans Ch. 10 v. 9
8: Acts Ch. 17 vs. 30, 31
9: Acts Ch. 2 vs. 37
10: Hebrews Ch.7 v. 25
11: Hebrews Ch.13 v. 5
12: 1 Cor. Ch. 15 vs. 51, 52
13: 1 Thess. Ch. 4 vs. 16, 17
14: Acts Ch. 16 v. 31
15: Romans Ch. 10 v. 13

What manner of Man is this!

1: Colossians Ch.1 vs. 15 – 17
2: Hebrews Ch.1 v. 3
3: 1 Corinthians Ch. 15 vs. 3 – 8
4: Acts Ch. 1 v. 8
5: Acts Ch. 1 vs. 9 – 11
6: 1 Timothy Ch.1 v. 15
7: Romans Ch.5 v. 6
8: Romans Ch.5 v. 8
9: Romans Ch.5 v. 9
10: Romans Ch.5 v. 11
11: John Ch. 21 v. 25
12: Romans Ch.6 v. 23
13: Isaiah Ch. 1 v. 18

Where is your Faith?

1: Romans Ch. 3 v. 23
2: Isaiah Ch. 59 v. 2
3: 1 Timothy Ch. 1 v. 15
4: Luke Ch. 19 v. 10
5: Ecclesiastes Ch. 7 v. 20
6: 1 John Ch.1 v. 9
7: Acts Ch. 3 v. 19
8: Acts Ch. 4 v. 12
9: John Ch. 14 v. 6
10: Isaiah Ch. 53 v .6
11: Romans Ch. 4 v. 25
12: Romans Ch. 5 v. 1
13: Revelation Ch. 3 v. 20
14: Hebrews Ch. 7 v. 25
15: Jude 24
16: 2 Corinthians Ch. 9 v. 8
17: Hebrews Ch. 8 v. 1
18: 1 Timothy Ch. 2 v. 5
19: Hebrews Ch.7 v.25
20: 1 John Ch. 2 v. 1
21: Hebrews Ch. 13 v. 5
22: 2 Corinthians Ch. 5 v. 17

The Hour is Coming

1: Mark Ch.8 v. 36

2: Proverbs Ch.1 v. 24

3: Isaiah Ch.65 v. 12

4: John Ch.5 v. 40

5: Genesis Ch.6 v. 3

6: Psalm 89 v. 48

7: Hebrews Ch.9 v. 27

8: John Ch.5 vs. 28, 29

9: Matthew Ch.25 v. 34

10: Matthew Ch.25 v. 41

How can You be Saved?

1: Romans Ch.3 v. 10

2: Romans Ch.3 v. 23

3: Romans Ch.6 v. 23

4: Luke Ch.18 v. 26

5: John Ch.14 v. 6

Knocking and Calling

1: Revelation Ch.3 v. 20

2: Hebrews Ch.4 v. 7

3: 2 Corinthians Ch.6 v. 2